LOCO-HAULED TRAVEL 1987-88

Neil Webster, Simon Greaves
and Robert Greengrass

Published by **Metro Enterprises Ltd.**, 48 Southcliffe Drive, Baildon, BD17 6QX
and Printed by Waddington & Sons (Printers) Ltd., Todmorden

ISBN 0-947773-09-6

LOCOMOTIVE WORKINGS

CLASSES 03, 08 & 09

Being by nature of their design essentially shunting locomotives, the uses for these classes on legitimate passenger duties (as opposed to shunt releases) are obviously limited. In the timetable period under review there are no regular booked workings on scheduled services, and the only likely uses would appear to be on railtours, at depot/station open days or following failures of either other locomotive types, multiple units or coaching stock at or adjacent to stations, depots or yards where a pilot duty is employed.

CLASS 20

All members of this class are now allocated to the Freight and Departmental sectors of BR and as such have no booked workings on scheduled services. The class remains tremendously popular with enthusiasts and are a popular choice for railtours, often covering routes not normally visited by the class. The nominal speed restriction of 60 mph for these locomotives restricts the scope for their use on passenger services vice other power, and it would appear that during the timetable period under review that the best opportunities to travel behind these locomotives may occur in the event of overhead line difficulties on the West Coast Main Line, particularly between Crewe and Preston.

CLASS 26

This class is now the basic Scottish Region low powered locomotive for freight, departmental & parcels working, and as such passenger workings are now very rare. There are no booked workings on scheduled services in the timetable period under review, and the best opportunities for workings would appear to be vice other power in emergencies on services between Edinburgh and Dundee, Cardenden or Carstairs, or Glasgow Central and Carlisle (Via Kilmarnock).

CLASS 31/1

Due to lack of suitable train heating equipment this sub class has no booked duties on scheduled trains in the timetable period under review. However, they are very frequently used as substitutes for the unavailability of other power and as such appear on a reasonably regular basis on many routes throughout the Eastern, London Midland and Western Regions.

CLASS 31/4

These locomotives remain the mainstay of Provincial sector cross country routes in the Midlands and North, but the routes which they work may begin to be infiltrated by Sprinter Units during the latter part of the timetable period under review. However, continued problems with both these units and the various railbus types may very well grant a stay of execution to the introduction of such units and allow the class a swansong on passenger working.

IMMINGHAM DEPOT

31.401:	0610	Cleethorpes–Liverpool L.S.	
	1145	Liverpool L.S.–Sheffield	
	1422	Sheffield–Liverpool L.S.	
	1745	Liverpool L.S.–Sheffield	
31.402:	1009	Sheffield–Harwich P.Q.	0720 from Blackpool N.
	1705	Harwich P.Q.–Wolverhampton	

31.403: 0734 SX Wolverhampton–Birmingham N.S.
0820 SX Birmingham N.S.–Norwich
1640 SX Norwich–Birmingham N.S.
31.404: 1039 SO Birmingham N.S.–Norwich
1715 SO Norwich–Yarmouth   1045 from Liverpool L.S.
1820 SO Yarmouth–Norwich
31.405: 0520 Wolverhampton–Harwich P.Q.
1320 Harwich P.Q.–Sheffield
1922 Sheffield–Liverpool L.S.
31.406: 0630 Liverpool L.S.–Sheffield
0922 Sheffield–Liverpool L.S.
1245 Liverpool L.S.–Sheffield
1522 Sheffield–Liverpool L.S.
1845 Liverpool L.S.–Sheffield
31.407: 0845 Liverpool L.S.–Sheffield
1122 Sheffield–Liverpool L.S.
1445 Liverpool L.S.–Sheffield
1722 Sheffield–Liverpool L.S.
2145 Liverpool L.S.–Sheffield
31.408: 0655 SX Sheffield–Liverpool L.S.
0722 SO Sheffield–Liverpool L.S.
1045 Liverpool L.S.–Norwich
31.409: 0750 SX Yarmouth–Liverpool L.S.
0850 SO Norwich–Sheffield   0805 from Yarmouth.
1645 Liverpool L.S.–Sheffield
2122 Sheffield–Liverpool L.S.
31.410: 0738 Liverpool L.S.–Sheffield
1022 Sheffield–Liverpool L.S.
1345 Liverpool L.S.–Sheffield
1622 Sheffield–Liverpool L.S.
1945 SX Liverpool L.S.–Sheffield
31.411: 0604 Sheffield–Liverpool L.S.
0945 Liverpool L.S.–Sheffield
1222 Sheffield–Liverpool L.S.
1545 Liverpool L.S.–Cleethorpes
31.412: 1552 SUN Liverpool L.S.–Sheffield
1858 SUN Sheffield–Liverpool L.S.
31.413: 1120 SUN Cleethorpes–Liverpool L.S.
1852 SUN Liverpool L.S.–Sheffield
2201 SUN Sheffield–Liverpool L.S.
31.414: 1252 SUN Liverpool L.S.–Sheffield
1700 SUN Sheffield–Liverpool L.S.
2052 SUN Liverpool L.S.–Sheffield
31.415: 0759 SUN Sheffield–Liverpool L.S.
1422 SUN Liverpool L.S.–Sheffield
1743 SUN Sheffield–Liverpool L.S.
31.416: 1052 SUN Liverpool L.S.–Sheffield
1538 SUN Sheffield–Liverpool L.S.
1952 SUN Liverpool L.S.–Sheffield
31.417: 1155 SUN Sheffield–Liverpool L.S.
1752 SUN Liverpool L.S.–Cleethorpes
31.418: 1310 SUN Norwich–Sheffield
1815 SUN Sheffield–Norwich
31.419: 1635 SUN Norwich–Birmingham N.S.

MARCH DEPOT

Readers should note that this depot is expected to lose its allocation of this sub class during the timetable period under review, probably either to Immingham, Stratford or Tinsley.

31.420:	0650	SO	King's Lynn–Cambridge
	1613		Cambridge–Birmingham N.S.
	2035	FO	Birmingham N.S.–Cambridge
31.421:	0603	SX	Cambridge–Birmingham N.S.
	1039	SX	Birmingham N.S.–Norwich
	1715	SX	Norwich–Yarmouth	1045 from Liverpool L.S.
	1820	SX	Yarmouth–Norwich
31.422:	0630	SO	Norwich–Yarmouth
	0700	SX	Norwich–Yarmouth
	0805	SO	Yarmouth–Norwich
	1327		Norwich–Birmingham N.S.
	1830		Birmingham N.S.–Norwich
31.423:	0630	SX	Norwich–Yarmouth
	0810	SX	Yarmouth–Norwich
	1127		Norwich–Birmingham N.S.
	1620		Birmingham N.S.–Norwich
31.424:	0928		Ipswich–Birmingham N.S.
	1420		Birmingham N.S.–Ipswich
31.425:	0727		Norwich–Birmingham N.S.
	1220		Birmingham N.S.–Cambridge
	2151	FO	Cambridge–King's Lynn	2035 from Liverpool St.
31.426:	0734	SO	Wolverhampton–Birmingham N.S.
	0821	SO	Birmingham N.S.–Norwich
	1640	SO	Norwich–Birmingham N.S.
31.427:	1720	SUN	Birmingham N.S.–Norwich
31.428:	2255	SUN	Norwich–Ipswich
31.429:	1322	SUN	Ipswich–Birmingham N.S.
	1830	SUN	Birmingham N.S.–Ipswich

DMU REPLACEMENT DIAGRAMS

The following diagrams are expected to operate until further notice in lieu of Sprinter/Pacer units. These diagrams may be subject to alteration or amendment at short notice depending upon unit availability.

31.451:	0649	Burton-on-Trent–Sheffield
	0755	Sheffield–Ipswich
	1602	Ipswich–Sheffield
31.452:	0525	Cambridge–Birmingham N.S.
	1540	Birmingham N.S.–Cambridge
	1913	Cambridge–Peterborough
	2110	Peterborough–Cambridge

CLASSES 33/0 & 33/2

The workings for these sub classes remain largely unchanged from those in the previous timetable, but it must be stressed that the introduction of class 155 dmus to some turns is imminent within the course of the current timetable. When this occurs this may result in amended locomotive diagrams for the remaining locomotive hauled services and hence readers should be aware of this possibility. A number of further withdrawals of these locomotives can be expected before May 1988.

33.001:	0605		Salisbury–Portsmouth Hbr.	
	1010		Portsmouth Hbr.–Bristol T.M.	
	1405		Bristol T.M.–Portsmouth Hbr.	1305 from Cardiff C.
	1810		Portsmouth Hbr.–Bristol T.M.	
33.002:	0550	SO	Portsmouth Hbr.–Bristol T.M.	
	1012	SO	Bristol T.M.–Cardiff C.	0656 from Portsmouth Hbr.

	1206	SO	Cardiff C.–Bristol T.M.	
	1451	SO	Bristol T.M.–Cardiff C.	1210 from Portsmouth Hbr.
	1626	SO	Cardiff C.–Bristol T.M.	
	1810		Bristol T.M.–Portsmouth Hbr.	1605 from Swansea.
33.003:	0245	SX	Waterloo–Portsmouth Hbr.	
	0810		Portsmouth Hbr.–Bristol T.M.	
	1205		Bristol T.M.–Portsmouth Hbr.	0950 from Swansea.
	1610		Portsmouth Hbr.–Bristol T.M.	
	1920	SX	Bristol T.M.–Portsmouth Hbr.	1810 from Cardiff C.
	2100	SO	Bristol T.M.–Cardiff C.	1810 from Portsmouth Hbr.
33.004:	0550	SX	Portsmouth Hbr.–Bristol T.M.	
	1105	SX	Bristol T.M.–Portsmouth Hbr.	1010 from Cardiff C.
	1510	SX	Portsmouth Hbr.–Bristol T.M.	
	2100	SX	Bristol T.M.–Cardiff C.	1810 from Portsmouth Hbr.
33.005:	0550	SO	Cardiff C.–Bristol T.M.	
	0756	SO	Bristol T.M.–Portsmouth Hbr.	0630 from Cardiff C.
	1210	SO	Portsmouth Hbr.–Bristol T.M.	
	1615		Bristol T.M.–Weymouth	
	1935		Weymouth–Bristol T.M.	
	2335	SX	Bristol T.M.–Cardiff C.	2025 from Portsmouth Hbr.
33.006:	0500		Bristol T.M.–Yeovil P.M.	
	0655		Yeovil P.M.–Bristol T.M.	
	1008	SO	Bristol T.M.–Portsmouth Hbr.	
	1012	SX	Bristol T.M.–Cardiff C.	0656 from Portsmouth Hbr.
	1208	SX	Cardiff C.–Bristol T.M.	
	1354	SX	Bristol T.M.–Cardiff C.	1110 from Portsmouth Hbr.
	1410	SO	Portsmouth Hbr.–Bristol T.M.	
	1510	SX	Cardiff C.–Bristol T.M.	
	1718	SX	Bristol T.M.–Portsmouth Hbr.	1620 from Cardiff C.
	2125	SX	Portsmouth Hbr.–Salisbury	
	2207	SO	Bristol T.M.–Cardiff C.	
33.007:	0702	SX	Salisbury–Eastleigh	
	0903	SO	Bristol T.M.–Portsmouth Hbr.	0800 from Cardiff C.
	1310		Portsmouth Hbr.–Bristol T.M.	
	1650		Bristol T.M.–Cardiff C.	1410 from Portsmouth Hbr.
	1810		Cardiff C.–Bristol T.M.	
	2008	SO	Bristol T.M.–Cardiff C.	1710 from Portsmouth Hbr.
33.008:	0703	SO	Bristol T.M.–Portsmouth Hbr.	0550 from Cardiff C.
	1110	SO	Portsmouth Hbr.–Bristol T.M.	
	1610	SO	Bristol T.M.–Brighton	1510 from Cardiff C.
33.009:	0756	SX	Bristol T.M.–Portsmouth Hbr.	0630 from Cardiff C.
	1210	SX	Portsmouth Hbr.–Bristol T.M.	
	1610	SX	Bristol T.M.–Brighton	1510 from Cardiff C.
33.010:	0830		Brighton–Bristol T.M.	
	1305	SX	Bristol T.M.–Portsmouth Hbr.	1208 from Cardiff C.
	1505	SO	Bristol T.M.–Portsmouth Hbr.	1400 from Cardiff C.
	1710	SX	Portsmouth Hbr.–Bristol T.M.	
	2025*	SO	Portsmouth Hbr.–Bristol T.M.	
	2025*	SO	Portsmouth Hbr.–Bristol T.M.	
	2025*	SO	Portsmouth Hbr.–Westbury	
	2145	SX	Bristol T.M.–Southampton C.	
	2247*	SO	Westbury–Salisbury	
33.011:	0656		Portsmouth Hbr.–Bristol T.M.	
	1045		Bristol T.M.–Cardiff C.	0810 from Portsmouth Hbr.
	1305		Cardiff C.–Bristol T.M.	
	1505	SX	Bristol T.M.–Portsmouth Hbr.	1400 from Cardiff C.
	1718	SO	Bristol T.M.–Portsmouth Hbr.	1620 from Cardiff C.
	2025	SX	Portsmouth Hbr.–Bristol T.M.	
	2125	SO	Portsmouth Hbr.–Salisbury	

33.012:	0703	SX	Bristol T.M.–Portsmouth Hbr.	0550 from Cardiff C.
	1110	SX	Portsmouth Hbr.–Bristol T.M.	
	1451	SX	Bristol T.M.–Cardiff C.	1210 from Portsmouth Hbr.
	1620	SX	Cardiff C.–Bristol T.M.	
	2015	SX	Bristol T.M.–Portsmouth Hbr.	
33.013:	0903	SX	Bristol T.M.–Portsmouth Hbr.	0800 from Cardiff C.
33.014:	0155		Southampton C.–Bristol T.M.	
	0859	SX	Bristol T.M.–Cardiff C.	0550 from Portsmouth Hbr.
	1010	SX	Cardiff C.–Bristol T.M.	
	1305	SO	Bristol T.M.–Portsmouth Hbr.	1206 from Cardiff C.
	1710	SO	Portsmouth Hbr.–Bristol T.M.	
33.015:	0716	SX	Salisbury–Waterloo	
	1410	SX	Waterloo–Salisbury	
	1725	SX	Salisbury–Waterloo	
	2252	SX	Waterloo–Eastleigh	
33.016:	0624		Fareham–Eastleigh	
33.017:	0703	SO	Salisbury–Eastleigh	
33.018:	0245	SO	Waterloo–Portsmouth Hbr.	
33.019:	0550	SO	Exeter St. D.–Hove	2 x 33
	1112	SO	Brighton–Exeter St. D.	2 x 33
	2015	SO	Bristol T.M.–Portsmouth Hbr.	
33.020:	1105	SO	Bristol T.M.–Portsmouth Hbr.	1010 from Cardiff C.
	1510	SO	Portsmouth Hbr.–Bristol T.M.	
	1920	SO	Bristol T.M.–Portsmouth Hbr.	1810 from Cardiff C.
33.021:	1610	SO	Waterloo–Salisbury	
	1920	SO	Salisbury–Basingstoke	
33.022:	2210	SO	Waterloo–Salisbury	
33.023:	0915*	SUN	Portsmouth Hbr.–Salisbury	
	0924*	SUN	Portsmouth Hbr.–Westbury	
	1006*	SUN	Bristol T.M.–Portsmouth Hbr.	
	1046*	SUN	Westbury–Portsmouth Hbr.	
	1119*	SUN	Salisbury–Portsmouth Hbr.	
	1415	SUN	Portsmouth Hbr.–Bristol T.M.	
	1918	SUN	Bristol T.M.–Portsmouth Hbr.	1806 from Cardiff C.
33.024:	1250	SUN	Bristol T.M.–Cardiff C.	1200 from Westbury.
	1453	SUN	Cardiff C.–Bristol T.M.	
	1705	SUN	Bristol T.M.–Cardiff C.	1415 from Portsmouth Hbr.
	1902	SUN	Cardiff C.–Bristol T.M.	
33.025:	0315	SUN	Waterloo–Portsmouth & S.	
	1515	SUN	Portsmouth Hbr.–Bristol T.M.	
	1902	SUN	Bristol T.M.–Cardiff C.	1615 from Portsmouth Hbr.
33.026:	0723	SUN	Portsmouth Hbr.–Salisbury	
	1017	SUN	Salisbury–Brighton	
	1612	SUN	Brighton–Bristol T.M.	
	2303	SUN	Bristol T.M.–Cardiff C.	2015 from Portsmouth Hbr.
33.027:	1015	SUN	Cardiff C.–Bristol T.M.	
	1600	SUN	Bristol T.M.–Portsmouth Hbr.	* 1453 from Cardiff
	2015	SUN	Portsmouth Hbr.–Bristol T.M.	
33.028:	1012*	SUN	Brighton–Bristol T.M.	
	1120*	SUN	Bristol T.M.–Westbury	1015 from Cardiff C.
	1400*	SUN	Westbury–Bristol T.M.	
	1805	SUN	Bristol T.M.–Brighton	1655 from Cardiff C.
33.029:	1803*	SUN	Salisbury–Waterloo	
	1820*	SUN	Salisbury–Waterloo	
	2110+	SUN	Waterloo–Yeovil Jn.	+ 7/2–20/3
	2210+	SUN	Waterloo–Salisbury	+ Not 7/2–20/3
33.030:	0920	SUN	Bristol T.M.–Westbury	0815 from Cardiff C.
	1700	SUN	Bristol T.M.–Portsmouth Hbr.	1600 from Cardiff C.
	2242	SUN	Portsmouth Hbr.–Salisbury	

33.031:	1430*	SUN	Salisbury–Portsmouth Hbr.	
	1815	SUN	Portsmouth Hbr.–Bristol T.M.	
	2155	SUN	Bristol T.M.–Portsmouth & S.	2100 from Cardiff C.
33.032:	0200	SUN	Waterloo–Fareham	
33.033:	0915*	SUN	Portsmouth Hbr.–Bristol T.M.	
	1110+	SUN	Cardiff C.–Bristol T.M.	+ From 7/2
	1450*	SUN	Bristol T.M.–Cardiff C.	
	1655	SUN	Cardiff C.–Bristol T.M.	
33.034:	0815*	SUN	Cardiff C.–Bristol T.M.	
	1012*	SUN	Brighton–Westbury	
	1405*	SUN	Bristol T.M.–Portsmouth Hbr.	
	1444*	SUN	Westbury–Portsmouth Hbr.	
	1505*	SUN	Bristol T.M.–Portsmouth Hbr.	1400 from Cardiff C.
	1915	SUN	Portsmouth Hbr.–Bristol T.M.	
33.035:	0346*	SUN	Salisbury–Yeovil Jn.	0130 from Waterloo.
	0723*	SUN	Yeovil Jn.–Salisbury	
33.036:	1400	SUN	Cardiff C.–Bristol T.M.	
	1600	SUN	Bristol T.M.–Cardiff C.	
	1806	SUN	Cardiff C.–Bristol T.M.	
	2003	SUN	Bristol T.M.–Cardiff C.	1612 from Brighton.
	2305	SUN	Cardiff C.–Bristol T.M.	
33.037:	0915*	SUN	Portsmouth Hbr.–Salisbury	
	0915*	SUN	Portsmouth Hbr.–Westbury	
	1012*	SUN	Brighton–Salisbury	
	1208*	SUN	Bristol T.M.–Portsmouth Hbr.	
	1247*	SUN	Westbury–Portsmouth Hbr.	
	1324*	SUN	Salisbury–Portsmouth Hbr.	
	1615	SUN	Portsmouth Hbr.–Bristol T.M.	
	2010	SUN	Bristol T.M.–Portsmouth Hbr.	1902 from Cardiff C.
33.038:	0345	SUN	London Br.–Dover W.D.	

CLASS 33/1

Workings for this sub class follow a similar pattern to recent years, being concentrated on the South Western Division of the Southern Region. Many of the trains listed forming the Waterloo to Weymouth service are hauled or pushed by emu stock between Waterloo and Bournemouth or vice–versa.

33.101:	0433	SX	Eastleigh–Bournemouth	0245 from Waterloo.
	0716		Bournemouth–Weymouth	
	0833		Weymouth–Bournemouth	
	1016		Bournemouth–Weymouth	0832 from Waterloo.
	1132		Weymouth–Bournemouth	
	1316		Bournemouth–Weymouth	1132 from Waterloo.
	1432		Weymouth–Bournemouth	
	1616		Bournemouth–Weymouth	1432 from Waterloo.
	1733	SX	Weymouth–Bournemouth	
	1737	SO	Weymouth–Bournemouth	
	1916	SO	Bournemouth–Weymouth	1732 from Waterloo.
	1920	SX	Bournemouth–Weymouth	1730 from Waterloo.
	2100		Weymouth–Bournemouth	
	2300	SO	Bournemouth–Eastleigh	
	2302	SX	Bournemouth–Weymouth	2044 from Waterloo.
33.102:	0616		Bournemouth–Weymouth	
	0730	SX	Weymouth–Bournemouth	
	0732	SO	Weymouth–Bournemouth	2 x 33/1
	0856		Bournemouth–Weymouth	0644 from Waterloo.
	1032		Weymouth–Bournemouth	
	1216		Bournemouth–Weymouth	1032 from Waterloo.
	1332		Weymouth–Bournemouth	
	1516		Bournemouth–Weymouth	1332 from Waterloo.
	1631	SX	Weymouth–Bournemouth	

	1632	SO	Weymouth–Bournemouth	
	1816		Bournemouth–Weymouth	1632 from Waterloo.
	1946	SO	Weymouth–Bournemouth	
	1954	SX	Weymouth–Bournemouth	
	2116		Bournemouth–Weymouth	1932 from Waterloo.
	2338	SO	Weymouth–Dorchester S.	
33.103:	0049	MX	Eastleigh–Weymouth	2252 from Waterloo.
	0101	MO	Bournemouth–Weymouth	2244 from Waterloo.
	0609	SX	Weymouth–Bournemouth	
	0632	SO	Weymouth–Bournemouth	
	0757		Bournemouth–Weymouth	0540 from Waterloo.
	0932		Weymouth–Bournemouth	
	1116		Bournemouth–Weymouth	0932 from Waterloo.
	1228		Weymouth–Bournemouth	
	1416		Bournemouth–Weymouth	1232 from Waterloo.
	1532		Weymouth–Bournemouth	
	1716		Bournemouth–Weymouth	1532 from Waterloo.
	1854	SO	Weymouth–Bournemouth	
	1902	SX	Weymouth–Bournemouth	
	2016	SO	Bournemouth–Weymouth	1832 from Waterloo.
	2021	SX	Bournemouth–Weymouth	1832 from Waterloo.
	2253	SO	Weymouth–Eastleigh	
33.104:	0806	SX	Weymouth–Bournemouth	
	1746	SX	Bournemouth–Weymouth	
	2238	SX	Weymouth–Eastleigh	
33.105:	0612	SX	Salisbury–Waterloo	
	0810	SX	Waterloo–Salisbury	
33.106:	0635	SX	Basingstoke–Salisbury	
	0748	SO	Salisbury–Waterloo	
	0804	SX	Salisbury–Waterloo	
	1010		Waterloo–Salisbury	
	1210	SO	Salisbury–Waterloo	
	1315	SX	Salisbury–Waterloo	
	1410	SO	Waterloo–Salisbury	
	1600	SX	Clapham Jn.–Kensington O.	
	1612	SX	Kensington O.–Clapham Jn.	
	1625	SX	Clapham Jn.–Kensington O.	
	1637	SX	Kensington O.–Clapham Jn.	
	1650	SX	Clapham Jn.–Kensington O.	
	1703	SX	Kensington O.–Clapham Jn.	
	1715	SX	Clapham Jn.–Kensington O.	
	1727	SX	Kensington O.–Clapham Jn.	
	1732	SO	Salisbury–Waterloo	
	1810	SX	Waterloo–Yeovil Jn.	M.emu to Basingstoke
	2120	FSX	Yeovil Jn.–Salisbury	
	2120	FO	Yeovil Jn.–Basingstoke	
33.107:	0600	SO	Salisbury–Basingstoke	
	0737	SX	Salisbury–Sherborne	0635 from Basingstoke.
	0839	SO	Basingstoke–Salisbury	
	0845	SX	Sherborne–Waterloo	
	0944	SO	Salisbury–Waterloo	
	1210		Waterloo–Salisbury	
	1515	SX	Salisbury–Waterloo	
	1532	SO	Salisbury–Waterloo	
	1700	SX	Waterloo–Basingstoke	M.emu to Basingstoke
	1810	SO	Waterloo–Salisbury	
	2120	SO	Salisbury–Basingstoke	
	2223	FSX	Salisbury–Basingstoke	2120 from Yeovil Jn.
33.108:	0433	SO	Eastleigh–Bournemouth	0245 from Waterloo.
	0735	SX	Poole–Bournemouth	M.73.110
	0741	SO	Poole–Bournemouth	M.73.110
	1636	SX	Salisbury–Basingstoke	
	2302	SO	Bournemouth–Weymouth	2044 from Waterloo.

```
33.109:  0039  SUN  Eastleigh–Weymouth             2252 from Waterloo.
         0821+ SUN  Weymouth–Bournemouth          M.33.116 + From 27/3
         0848+ SUN  Weymouth–Bournemouth          + To 20/3
         1105+ SUN  Bournemouth–Weymouth          + To 20/3
         1118+ SUN  Bournemouth–Weymouth          + From 27/3
         1251  SUN  Weymouth–Bournemouth
         1505  SUN  Bournemouth–Weymouth          1244 from Waterloo.
         1630  SUN  Weymouth–Bournemouth
         1818  SUN  Bournemouth–Weymouth          1630 from Waterloo.
         1948  SUN  Weymouth–Bournemouth
         2118  SUN  Bournemouth–Weymouth          1930 from Waterloo.
         2242  SUN  Weymouth–Bournemouth
33.110:  0734  SUN  Basingstoke–Reading G.
         0850  SUN  Reading G.–Portsmouth Hbr.
         1103  SUN  Portsmouth Hbr.–Reading G.
         1350  SUN  Reading G.–Portsmouth Hbr.
         1603  SUN  Portsmouth Hbr.–Reading G.
         1850  SUN  Reading G.–Portsmouth Hbr.
         2103  SUN  Portsmouth Hbr.–Reading G.
33.111:  0758+ SUN  Eastleigh–Weymouth            + From 27/3
         0951+ SUN  Weymouth–Bournemouth          + Until 20/3
         1034+ SUN  Weymouth–Bournemouth          + From 27/3
         1205+ SUN  Bournemouth–Weymouth          + Until 20/3
         1305+ SUN  Bournemouth–Weymouth          + From 27/3
         1348+ SUN  Weymouth–Bournemouth          + Until 20/3
         1430* SUN  Weymouth–Bournemouth
         1605  SUN  Bournemouth–Weymouth          1344 from Waterloo.
         1726  SUN  Weymouth–Bournemouth
         1918  SUN  Bournemouth–Weymouth          1730 from Waterloo.
         2051  SUN  Weymouth–Bournemouth
         2305  SUN  Bournemouth–Weymouth          2044 from Waterloo.
33.112:  0559+ SUN  Bournemouth–Eastleigh         M.emu + From 27/3
         0715+ SUN  Eastleigh–Weymouth            + From 27/3
         0758* SUN  Eastleigh–Weymouth            + Until 20/3
         0951+ SUN  Weymouth–Bournemouth          + From 27/3
         1034+ SUN  Weymouth–Bournemouth          + Until 20/3
         1205+ SUN  Bournemouth–Weymouth          + From 27/3
         1305+ SUN  Bournemouth–Weymouth          + Until 20/3
         1348+ SUN  Weymouth–Bournemouth          + From 27/3
         1451* SUN  Weymouth–Bournemouth
         2018  SUN  Bournemouth–Weymouth          1830 from Waterloo.
         2348  SUN  Weymouth–Poole                + 4/10
33.113:  0739+ SUN  Poole–Bournemouth             + From 27/3 M.73.119
33.114:  0750  SUN  Reading G.–Eastleigh
33.115:  0906  SUN  Eastleigh–Portsmouth Hbr.     0750 from Reading G.
         1003  SUN  Portsmouth Hbr.–Reading G.
         1250  SUN  Reading G.–Portsmouth Hbr.
         1503  SUN  Portsmouth Hbr.–Reading G.
         1750  SUN  Reading G.–Portsmouth Hbr.
         2003  SUN  Portsmouth Hbr.–Reading G.
         2300  SUN  Reading G.–Basingstoke
33.116:  0739+ SUN  Poole–Bournemouth             + To 27/3 M.73.119
         0821+ SUN  Weymouth–Bournemouth          M.33.109 + From 27/3
         1018* SUN  Bournemouth–Weymouth          0830 from Waterloo.
         1018+ SUN  Bournemouth–Weymouth          + Until 20/3
         1140  SUN  Weymouth–Bournemouth
         1405  SUN  Bournemouth–Weymouth          1144 from Waterloo.
         1530  SUN  Weymouth–Bournemouth
         1705  SUN  Bournemouth–Weymouth          1444 from Waterloo.
         1851  SUN  Weymouth–Bournemouth
```

CLASSES 37/0 & 37/5

In the winter timetable period the scope for the use of these locomotives is limited by their lack of suitable train heating equipment. They may however appear in place of class 37/4 on routes where the use of larger power is precluded by reason of route availability. The only booked diagrams are as banking locomotives on the Lickey Incline as follows:

37.001: 2256 SX   Bromsgrove–Blackwell   B.47.538 (2 x 37)

It should be noted that the above turn is now booked for a Tinsley 37 and a WR 37 in multiple, rather than the 2 x WR 37s previously the norm.

37.002: 2256 SO   Bromsgrove–Blackwell   B.47.538

On Saturdays when engineering operations necessitate the diversion of the above train via Worcester Shrub Hill and Hartlebury, a pilot locomotive is usually attached at Worcester Shrub Hill vice the banker and works through to Birmingham New Street. This locomotive is often a class 37.

37.003: 2256 SUN Bromsgrove–Blackwell   B.47.571

CLASS 37/4

Workings for this sub class remain largely unchanged from the summer timetable, the main scheduled work being in Scotland and on the Cambrian lines.

CARDIFF DEPOT

37.401:	0714		Aberystwyth–Shrewsbury
	1847	SX	Shrewsbury–Aberystwyth 1540 from Euston.
37.402:	0950	SX	Swansea–Bristol T.M.
	1250	SX	Bristol T.M.–Swansea 1010 from Portsmouth Hbr.
	1605	SX	Swansea–Bristol T.M.
	1853	SX	Bristol T.M.–Cardiff C. 1610 from Portsmouth Hbr.
37.403:	1835		Cardiff C.–Crewe
37.404:	0620		Crewe–Cardiff C.
	1045		Cardiff C.–Crewe
	1719		Crewe–Cardiff C.
37.405:	1600	SUN	Cardiff C.–Bristol T.M.
	1802	SUN	Bristol T.M.–Cardiff C. 1515 from Portsmouth Hbr.
	2100	SUN	Cardiff C.–Bristol T.M.
	2208	SUN	Bristol T.M.–Cardiff C. 1915 from Portsmouth Hbr.
37.406:	1340	SUN	Crewe–Swansea
	1828	SUN	Swansea–Crewe

EASTFIELD DEPOT

37.407:	0540		Glasgow Q.S.–Fort William 2055 from Euston.
	1405		Fort William–Mallaig
	1550	SX	Mallaig–Fort William
	1550	SO	Mallaig–Glasgow Q.S.
	1740	SX	Fort William–Glasgow Q.S.
37.408:	0820		Glasgow Q.S.–Oban
	1300		Oban–Glasgow Q.S.
	1820	SX	Glasgow Q.S.–Oban
	1820	SO	Glasgow Q.S.–Oban
37.409:	0800		Oban–Glasgow Q.S.
	1220		Glasgow Q.S.–Oban
	1800		Oban–Glasgow Q.S.
37.410:	1005		Fort William–Mallaig
	1220		Mallaig–Fort William
	1415		Fort William–Glasgow Q.S.
37.411:	0950		Glasgow Q.S.–Fort William
	1610		Fort William–Mallaig
	1850		Mallaig–Fort William
	2105		Fort William–Mallaig

37.412:	1005	MFSX	Fort William–Mallaig
	1220	MFSX	Mallaig–Fort William
	1610	MFSX	Fort William–Mallaig
	1850	MFSX	Mallaig–Fort William
	2105	MFSX	Fort William–Mallaig
37.413:	2225	SX	Glasgow Q.S.–Mossend Yard	1740 from Fort William.
37.414:	0318		Mossend Yard–Glasgow Q.S.	2055 from Euston.
37.415:	2230	SUN	Glasgow Q.S.–Mossend Yard	1740 from Fort William.
37.416:	1750	SUN	Glasgow Q.S.–Fort William
37.417:	1740	SUN	Fort William–Glasgow Q.S.
37.418:	1800	SUN	Oban–Crianlarich
	2000	SUN	Crianlarich–Oban
37.419:	2230	SUN	Glasgow Q.S.–Mossend Yard	1740 from Fort William.

INVERNESS DEPOT

37.421:	0602	Thurso–Georgemas Jn.
	1034	Georgemas Jn.–Thurso
	1202	Thurso–Georgemas Jn.
	1534	Georgemas Jn.–Thurso
	1802	Thurso–Georgemas Jn.
	2134	Georgemas Jn.–Thurso
37.422:	0655	Inverness–Kyle of Lochalsh
	1130	Kyle of Lochalsh–Inverness
	1735	Inverness–Wick
37.423:	0600	Wick–Inverness
	1135	Inverness–Wick
	1800	Wick–Inverness
37.424:	0635	Inverness–Wick
	1200	Wick–Inverness
	1755	Inverness–Kyle of Lochalsh
37.425:	0710	Kyle of Lochalsh–Inverness
37.426:	1015	Inverness–Kyle of Lochalsh
	1710	Kyle of Lochalsh–Inverness

CLASSES 37/7 & 37/9

These freight sector RA7 variants of class 37 are not expected to see any use on passenger services during the current timetable period, other than perhaps on railtours and following failures of other motive power. Examples appearing from BREL Crewe Works after classified overhaul may appear in tandem with other motive power on services between Crewe and Cardiff Central for either the whole or part of the journey. This latter use of course depends upon the availability of suitable locomotives and other test train commitments.

CLASS 40

Other than on railtours, the last surviving member of this class in BR service is not expected to see much use on passenger workings as it is no longer able to heat passenger coaching stock. However, from time to time it does perform on scheduled services between Leeds and Carlisle, with a class 97/2 being provided for train heating purposes.

CLASS 45/0

The few surviving members of this sub class are mainly used in the Sheffield area on freight, parcels and departmental train duties. They are only expected to appear on passenger services on very rare occasions due to the unavailability of other motive power.

CLASS 45/1

Although all the surviving members of this sub class are nominally allocated to the parcels sector, the following diagram will apply until further notice as replacement for a Sprinter unit working. (Subject to alteration or cancellation at short notice).

45.101:	0725	SX	Nottingham–Leeds
	0742	SO	Nottingham–Leeds
	1027		Leeds–Nottingham
	1325		Nottingham–Leeds
	1627		Leeds–Nottingham
	1854		Nottingham–Leicester
	2210		Leicester–Sheffield

Occasional use is also made of this class on the Liverpool–Newcastle services which are diagrammed for Gateshead based class 47/4 (q.v.).

CLASSES 47/0 & 47/3

The limiting of the maximum speed of these classes to a nominal 75 or 60 mph has reduced the scope for the use of these locomotives on passenger train duties. However, they still appear with reasonable regularity vice other motive power, in particular hauling normally electrically motivated services at times of overhead line isolations.

CLASS 47/4

This class provides the staple booked power for the majority of diesel-hauled trains on BR.

GATESHEAD DEPOT

The Newcastle–Liverpool and vice versa turns shown below are almost exclusively operated by locomotives in pool PTPA (See Motive Power Pocket Book).

47.401:	0605		Newcastle–Liverpool L.S.	
	1303		Liverpool L.S.–Newcastle	
	1825		Newcastle–Liverpool L.S.	
47.402:	0715		Manchester V.–Liverpool L.S.	
	1103		Liverpool L.S.–Newcastle	
	1625		Newcastle–Liverpool L.S.	
47.403:	0903		Liverpool L.S.–Newcastle	
	1425		Newcastle–Liverpool L.S.	
47.404:	0703		Liverpool L.S.–Newcastle	
	1225		Newcastle–Liverpool L.S.	
	1858		Liverpool L.S.–Newcastle	
47.405:	0825		Newcastle–Liverpool L.S.	
	1503		Liverpool L.S.–Newcastle	
47.406:	1025		Newcastle–Liverpool L.S.	
	1703		Liverpool L.S.–Newcastle	
47.407:	0015	SUN	Liverpool L.S.–Crewe	
	0339	SUN	Crewe–Liverpool L.S.	2350 from Euston.
	0850	SUN	Liverpool L.S.–Newcastle	
	1450	SUN	Newcastle–Liverpool L.S.	
47.408:	1048	SUN	Liverpool L.S.–Newcastle	
	1650	SUN	Newcastle–Liverpool L.S.	
47.409:	1350	SUN	Liverpool L.S.–Newcastle	
	1930	SUN	Newcastle–Liverpool L.S.	
47.410:	1200	SUN	Newcastle–Liverpool L.S.	
	1942	SUN	Liverpool L.S.–Newcastle	
47.411:	1000	SUN	Newcastle–Liverpool L.S.	
	1742	SUN	Liverpool L.S.–Newcastle	
47.412:	0800	SUN	Newcastle–Liverpool L.S.	
	1550	SUN	Liverpool L.S.–Newcastle	
47.413:	0745	SO	Newcastle–Birmingham N.S.	
47.414:	1200	SX	Bristol T.M.–Cardiff C.	0830 from Brighton.
	1400	SX	Cardiff C.–Bristol T.M.	
	1648	FO	Bristol T.M.–Weston Super Mare	
	1750	FO	Weston Super Mare–Bristol T.M.	
47.415:	0715	SX	Dundee–Edinburgh	

47.416:	1855	SUN	Birmingham N.S.–Newcastle	1448 from Southampton C.
47.417:	1525*	SUN	York–Birmingham N.S.	0950 from Glasgow C.
47.418:	1518	SUN	Channelsea Jn.–Camden Road	D.86.132
	2014	SUN	Willesden WL Jn.–Stratford (London)	D.86.132
47.419:	1430	SUN	Edinburgh–Aberdeen	
	1835	SUN	Aberdeen–Edinburgh	

STRATFORD DEPOT

Note A: 13/12–7/2, from 27/3.

47.420:	0745	SX	King's Lynn–Cambridge	
	0800	SO	King's Lynn–Cambridge	
	0944		Cambridge–King's Lynn	0835 from Liverpool St.
	1100		King's Lynn–Cambridge	
	1344		Cambridge–King's Lynn	1235 from Liverpool St.
	1500		King's Lynn–Cambridge	
	1744	SO	Cambridge–King's Lynn	1635 from Liverpool St.
	1751	SX	Cambridge–King's Lynn	1635 from Liverpool St.
	1905	SX	King's Lynn–Cambridge	
	1940	SO	King's Lynn–Cambridge	
47.421:	0720	SX	Cambridge–King's Lynn	
	0726	SO	Cambridge–King's Lynn	
	0900		King's Lynn–Cambridge	
	1144		Cambridge–King's Lynn	1035 from Liverpool St.
	1300		King's Lynn–Cambridge	
	1544		Cambridge–King's Lynn	1435 from Liverpool St.
	1700	SO	King's Lynn–Cambridge	
	1735	SX	King's Lynn–Cambridge	
	1944	SO	Cambridge–King's Lynn	1835 from Liverpool St.
	1951	SX	Cambridge–King's Lynn	1835 from Liverpool St.
47.422:	2300	SO	Liverpool St.–Norwich	
47.423:	1018	SUN	Cambridge–King's Lynn	
	1500	SUN	King's Lynn–Cambridge	
	1807	SUN	Cambridge–King's Lynn	1635 from Liverpool St.
	1950	SUN	King's Lynn–Cambridge	
47.424:	0800	SUN	King's Lynn–Cambridge	
	1105	SUN	Cambridge–King's Lynn	0935 from Liverpool St.
	1300	SUN	King's Lynn–Cambridge	
	1605	SUN	Cambridge–King's Lynn	1435 from Liverpool St.
	1730	SUN	King's Lynn–Cambridge	
	1959	SUN	Cambridge–King's Lynn	1835 from Liverpool St.
47.425:	0920+	SUN	Liverpool St.–Harwich P.Q.	+ See Note A.
	1315+	SUN	Harwich P.Q.–Liverpool St.	+ See Note A.
47.426:	0650*	SUN	Norwich–Colchester	
	1033*	SUN	Colchester–Norwich	
47.427:	0900*	SUN	Liverpool St.–Norwich	
47.428:	0650*	SUN	Norwich–Liverpool St.	
47.429:	0951	SO	Wolverhampton–Shrewsbury	0740 from Euston.
	1133	SO	Shrewsbury–Wolverhampton	
	1357	SO	Wolverhampton–Shrewsbury	1140 from Euston.
	1531	SO	Shrewsbury–Wolverhampton	
	1755	SO	Wolverhampton–Shrewsbury	1540 from Euston.
	2155	SO	Wolverhampton–Shrewsbury	1940 from Euston.

CREWE DEPOT

47.430:	2117	SO	Birmingham N.S.–Paddington	1920 from Manchester P.
47.431:	1215	SO	Birmingham N.S.–Plymouth	0720 from Glasgow C.
47.432:	0015	MX	Crewe–Holyhead	2200 from Euston.
	0021	MO	Crewe–Holyhead	2200 from Euston.
	0605		Holyhead–Crewe	

	0937	Crewe–Holyhead	0755 from Coventry.
	1255	Holyhead–Crewe	
	1831	Crewe–Holyhead	1617 from Euston.
47.433:	0856	Holyhead–Crewe	
	1347	Crewe–Holyhead	1130 from Euston.
	1710	Holyhead–Crewe	
47.434:	0714	Holyhead–Crewe	
	1158	Crewe–Holyhead	0930 from Euston.
	1615	Holyhead–Crewe	
	2103	Crewe–Holyhead	1850 from Euston.
47.435:	0115	Holyhead–Crewe	
	0800	Crewe–Cardiff C.	0515 from Holyhead.
	1300	Cardiff C.–Holyhead	
47.436:	0305	Manchester P.–Crewe	
47.437:	0735	Manchester V.–Preston	
	2157	SO	Preston–Manchester V.	1850 from Glasgow C.
	2219	SX	Preston–Manchester V.	1920 from Glasgow C.
47.438:	0620	Blackpool N.–Preston	
	1338	SO	Blackpool N.–Preston	
	1524	SO	Preston–Blackpool N.	1200 from Euston.
	1901	Preston–Manchester V.	1550 from Glasgow C.
47.439:	1615	SO	Liverpool L.S.–Poole	
47.440:	1025	Manchester V.–Preston	
	1214	Preston–Blackpool N.	0900 from Euston.
	1422	SX	Blackpool N.–Preston	
	1630	Blackpool N.–Preston	
	1928	Preston–Blackpool N.	1630 from Euston.
47.441:	0950	Blackpool N.–Preston	
	1524	SX	Preston–Blackpool N.	1200 from Euston.
	1940	SX	Preston–Barrow in Furness	
	2053	SO	Preston–Manchester V.	
	2149	SX	Barrow in Furness–Preston	
47.442:	2053	SX	Preston–Manchester V.	
47.443:	2244	Preston–Blackpool N.	1930 from Euston.
47.444:	0720	Blackpool N.–Sheffield	
	1156	Sheffield–Manchester P.	0720 from Harwich P.Q.
	1527	Manchester P.–Harwich P.Q.	
47.445:	0720	Harwich P.Q.–Sheffield	
	1822	Sheffield–Blackpool N.	1320 from Harwich P.Q.
47.446:	0625	SX	Poole–Manchester P.	
	0633	SO	Poole–Manchester P.	
	1615	SX	Liverpool L.S.–Poole	
47.447:	0834	Poole–Reading G.	
	1240	SX	Reading G.–Birmingham N.S.	1038 from Poole.
	1240	SO	Reading G.–Birmingham N.S.	1040 from Poole.
	1555	Birmingham N.S.–Plymouth	1050 from Glasgow C.
47.448:	0030	Plymouth–Paddington	2135 from Penzance.
	1034	Reading G.–Birmingham N.S.	0834 from Poole.
	1411	Birmingham N.S.–Poole	0850 from Glasgow C.
47.449:	1038	Poole–Reading G.	
	1442	Reading G.–Manchester P.	1238 from Poole.
47.450:	0808	Manchester P.–Poole	
	1458	Poole–Reading G.	
	1826	Reading G.–Poole	1410 from Liverpool L.S.
47.451:	0603	SX	Nottingham–St. Pancras	
	1730	SX	St. Pancras–Derby	
47.452:	1410	SO	Liverpool L.S.–Reading G.	
	1933	SO	Reading G.–Birmingham N.S.	1732 from Poole.

47.453:	0709	SX	Shrewsbury–Wolverhampton	
	0951	SX	Wolverhampton–Shrewsbury	0740 from Euston.
	1133	SX	Shrewsbury–Wolverhampton	
	1357	SX	Wolverhampton–Shrewsbury	1140 from Euston.
	1531	SX	Shrewsbury–Wolverhampton	
	1915	SX	Wolverhampton–Shrewsbury	1710 from Euston.
	2155	SX	Wolverhampton–Shrewsbury	1940 from Euston.
47.454:	0645		Wolverhampton–Poole	
	1238		Poole–Reading G.	
	1655		Reading G.–Birmingham N.S.	1458 from Poole.
47.455:	1455	SO	Birmingham N.S.–Newcastle	1040 from Poole.
47.456:	0740*	SUN	Liverpool L.S.–Crewe	
	0755*	SUN	Liverpool L.S.–Crewe	
	1146*	SUN	Liverpool L.S.–Crewe	
	1159*	SUN	Liverpool L.S.–Crewe	
	1350	SUN	Crewe–Liverpool L.S.	1050 from Euston.
47.457:	1231	SUN	Wolverhampton–Shrewsbury	0940 from Euston.
	1426	SUN	Shrewsbury–Wolverhampton	
	1733	SUN	Shrewsbury–Wolverhampton	
	1928	SUN	Wolverhampton–Shrewsbury	1710 from Euston.
46.457:	2228	SUN	Wolverhampton–Shrewsbury	2010 from Euston.
47.458:	1715	SUN	Birmingham N.S.–Edinburgh	1040 from Penzance.
47.459:	1345	SUN	Edinburgh–Birmingham N.S.	1030 from Aberdeen.
47.460:	0900	SUN	Paddington–Wolverhampton	
47.461:	1117	SUN	Manchester P.–Paddington	
	1810	SUN	Paddington–Birmingham N.S.	
47.462:	0900	SUN	Birmingham N.S.–Llandudno Junction	
	1300*	SUN	Llandudno Junction–Crewe	
	1321*	SUN	Llandudno Junction–Crewe	
47.463:	1250	SUN	Plymouth–Birmingham N.S.	1040 from Penzance.
	2215	SUN	Birmingham N.S.–Bristol T.M.	1720 from Glasgow C.
47.464:	0030	SUN	Manchester P.–Stafford	D.86.266
	0249	SUN	Stafford–Manchester P.	
	0935	SUN	Manchester P.–Birmingham N.S.	
47.465:	0045	SUN	Holyhead–Crewe	
	0529+	SUN	Warrington BQ–Crewe	+1/11–27/12 D.86.445
	1154	SUN	Crewe–Holyhead	0850 from Euston.
	1656	SUN	Holyhead–Crewe	
47.466:	1352	SUN	Holyhead–Crewe	
	2124	SUN	Crewe–Holyhead	1900 from Euston.
47.467:	0412+	SUN	Warrington BQ–Crewe	+1/11–27/12 D.87.044
	1250+	SUN	Crewe–Warrington BQ	+1/11–27/12 D.86.448
	1425+	SUN	Warrington BQ–Crewe	+1/11–27/12 D.86.429
47.468:	0033	SUN	Crewe–Holyhead	2150 from Euston.
47.469:	1254*	SUN	Holyhead–Crewe	
	1305*	SUN	Holyhead–Crewe	
	1922	SUN	Crewe–Holyhead	1700 from Euston.
47.470:	0938*	SUN	Liverpool L.S.–Crewe	
	0958*	SUN	Liverpool L.S.–Crewe	
	1202	SUN	Stafford–Manchester P.	0930 from Euston.
	1418	SUN	Manchester P.–Stafford	
47.471:	0932	SUN	Poole–Liverpool L.S.	
47.472:	1130	SUN	Manchester P.–Stafford	
47.473:	0835*	SUN	Liverpool L.S.–Crewe	
	0845*	SUN	Liverpool L.S.–Crewe	
	1148	SUN	Crewe–Liverpool L.S.	0810 from Euston.
47.474:	1037*	SUN	Liverpool L.S.–Crewe	
	1042*	SUN	Liverpool L.S.–Crewe	

	1429*	SUN	Liverpool L.S.–Crewe	
	1439*	SUN	Liverpool L.S.–Crewe	
47.475:	2149	SUN	Barrow in Furness–Preston	
47.476:	0830*	SUN	Birmingham N.S.–Preston	
47.477:	1030	SUN	Manchester P.–Stafford	
	1400	SUN	Stafford–Manchester P.	1130 from Euston.
47.478:	1519	SUN	Blackpool N.–Preston	
	1950+	SUN	Preston–Blackpool N.	
	2240	SUN	Preston–Blackpool N.	1930 from Euston.
47.479:	1406+	SUN	Manchester V.–Preston	
47.480:	0850	SUN	Manchester P.–Stafford	
	1300	SUN	Manchester P.–Birmingham N.S.	
	1925	SUN	Birmingham N.S.–Poole	1440 from Newcastle.
47.481:	1132	SUN	Poole–Birmingham N.S.	
	1821	SUN	Birmingham N.S.–Poole	0950 from Edinburgh.
47.482:	0820	SUN	Manchester P.–Stafford	
	1305	SUN	Manchester P.–Stafford	
47.483:	0948*	SUN	Blackpool N.–Preston	
	1019*	SUN	Blackpool N.–Preston	
	1802	SUN	Preston–Blackpool N.	1430 from Euston.
	1947	SUN	Blackpool N.–Preston	
	2256	SUN	Preston–Manchester V.	1945 from Glasgow C.
47.484:	1302*	SUN	Liverpool L.S.–Poole	
	1319*	SUN	Liverpool L.S.–Poole	
47.485:	1448	SUN	Southampton C.–Birmingham N.S.	
47.486:	1215	SUN	Derby–St. Pancras	
47.487:	1620	SUN	St. Pancras–Nottingham	
47.488:	1440	SUN	Newcastle–Birmingham N.S.	

Note: Turns 47.489 to 47.498 are deliberately left blank.

INVERNESS DEPOT

Note the diagrams from this depot now cover turns over the Settle & Carlisle route.

47.499:	0714		Edinburgh–Carstairs	
	1346	SO	Carstairs–Edinburgh	
	1544	SO	Edinburgh–Carstairs	
	1717	SO	Carstairs–Edinburgh	
	1844		Edinburgh–Carstairs	
	2144		Carstairs–Edinburgh	
47.500:	0736	SX	Edinburgh–Glasgow Q.S.	
	1333	SX	Glasgow Q.S.–Inverness	
	2340	SX	Inverness–Glasgow Q.S.	T.47.511
47.501:	0933		Glasgow Q.S.–Inverness	
	1430		Inverness–Edinburgh	
	2304*	SO	Edinburgh–Carstairs	
	2344*	SO	Edinburgh–Carstairs	
47.502:	1340		Aberdeen–Inverness	
	1800		Inverness–Aberdeen	
	2055		Aberdeen–Inverness	
47.503:	0500		Inverness–Aberdeen	
	0740		Aberdeen–Inverness	
	1032	SO	Inverness–Aberdeen	
	1225	SX	Inverness–Glasgow Q.S.	
	1540	SO	Aberdeen–Inverness	
	1803	SX	Glasgow Q.S.–Inverness	
	2055	SO	Inverness–Aberdeen	
47.504:	0600		Inverness–Aberdeen	
	1755	SO	Aberdeen–Inverness	
	2140	SX	Perth–Carstairs	

47.505:	0459	SO	Carstairs–Edinburgh
	0542	SX	Carstairs–Edinburgh	2345 from Euston.
	1125		Edinburgh–Inverness
	1820		Inverness–Glasgow Q.S.
47.506:	0740		Glasgow C.–Carlisle
	1155		Carlisle–Glasgow C.
	1545		Glasgow C.–Carlisle
47.507:	0630		Carlisle–Leeds
	1042		Leeds–Carlisle
	1615		Carlisle–Leeds
47.508:	0842		Leeds–Carlisle
	1237		Carlisle–Leeds
	1625		Leeds–Carlisle
47.509:	0424		Carlisle–Glasgow C.	2300 from Euston.
	0823		Glasgow C.–Stranraer Hbr.
	1425		Stranraer Hbr.–Glasgow C.
	2153		Glasgow C.–Stranraer Hbr.
47.510:	0700		Stranraer Hbr.–Glasgow C.
	1223	SX	Glasgow C.–Stranraer Hbr.
	1835	SX	Stranraer Hbr.–Glasgow C.
	2310*	SO	Glasgow C.–Carlisle
47.511:	0340		Perth–Stirling	T.47.500 or 47.520
	0548		Stirling–Edinburgh
	1140		Edinburgh–Carstairs
	1501	SX	Carstairs–Edinburgh	0855 from Euston.
	1609	SO	Carstairs–Edinburgh
	1744	SX	Edinburgh–Carstairs
	1859	SX	Carstairs–Edinburgh
	1955	SO	Edinburgh–Aberdeen	1859 from Carstairs.
47.512:	0710		Edinburgh–Inverness
	1432		Inverness–Aberdeen
	1755	SX	Aberdeen–Inverness
	2055	SX	Inverness–Aberdeen
47.513:	0625	SX	Aberdeen–Inverurie
	0733	SX	Inverurie–Aberdeen
47.514:	0435		Aberdeen–Inverness
	0832		Inverness–Aberdeen
	1140		Aberdeen–Inverness
	1700		Inverness–Edinburgh
	2325	SX	Edinburgh–Inverness
	2325	SO	Edinburgh–Perth
47.515:	0840		Inverness–Glasgow Q.S.
	1555		Glasgow Q.S.–Arbroath
	1924		Arbroath–Dundee
47.516:	0459	SX	Carstairs–Edinburgh
47.517:	0418	SO	Mossend Yard–Inverness	2230 from Euston.
	1225	SO	Inverness–Glasgow Q.S.
	1803	SO	Glasgow Q.S.–Inverness
47.518:	0700	SO	Dundee–Carstairs
	1501	SO	Carstairs–Edinburgh	0840 from Euston.
	1744	SO	Edinburgh–Carstairs
47.519:	0950*	SUN	Glasgow C.–Edinburgh
	1614*	SUN	Edinburgh–Carstairs	T.47.601
	1808*	SUN	Carstairs–Edinburgh
	1939	SUN	Edinburgh–Carstairs
47.520:	1310	SUN	Aberdeen–Inverness
	2340	SUN	Inverness–Glasgow Q.S.	T.47.511
47.521:	0420*	SUN	Carlisle–Glasgow C.	1840 from Plymouth.
	0513*	SUN	Carlisle–Glasgow C.	1840 from Plymouth.

47.522:	1540	SUN	Inverness–Aberdeen
	2010	SUN	Aberdeen–Inverness
47.523:	1655	SUN	Glasgow Q.S.–Inverness
47.524:	1540	SUN	Aberdeen–Inverness
	1840	SUN	Inverness–Aberdeen
47.525:	1650	SUN	Inverness–Glasgow Q.S.
47.526:	0322+	SUN	Warrington BQ–Crewe
	1112*	SUN	Warrington BQ–Crewe
	1455*	SUN	Crewe–Preston
	2004	SUN	Lancaster–Barrow in Furness
	2149	SUN	Barrow in Furness–Preston
47.527:	1352*	SUN	Carlisle–Glasgow C.
	1745*	SUN	Glasgow C.–Carlisle
47.528:	0340+	SUN	Carlisle–Glasgow C.
	0700+	SUN	Glasgow C.–Edinburgh
	0746+	SUN	Glasgow C.–Edinburgh
47.529:	2355	SUN	Edinburgh–Carstairs
47.530:	1730	SUN	Inverness–Edinburgh
	2325	SUN	Edinburgh–Inverness
47.531:	2140	SUN	Perth–Carstairs
47.532:	2306	SUN	Carstairs–Edinburgh

47.526 notes:
+1/11–27/12 D.87.045
D.86.262
D.86.445
1630 from Euston.

47.528 notes:
+ From 8/11
+ From 3/1
+ 8/11–27/12

WESTERN REGION

Note the workings to Shrewsbury, York and Holyhead formerly covered by Bescot and Crewe based locomotives.

47.533:	0920		Channelsea Jn.–Camden Road	D.86.118
	1022		Mitre Bridge Jn.–Dover W.D.	0740 from Manchester P.
	1355	SO	Dover W.D.–Willesden WL Jn.	
	1355	SX	Dover W.D.–Willesden WL Jn.	
	1923		Mitre Bridge Jn.–Brighton	1640 from Manchester P.
47.534:	0635		Brighton–Willesden WL Jn.	
	1055		Mitre Bridge Jn.–Brighton	0720 from Liverpool L.S.
	1322		Brighton–Willesden WL Jn.	
	1531		Mitre Bridge Jn.–Brighton	1155 from Manchester P.
	1825		Brighton–Willesden WL Jn.	
47.535:	0745		Mitre Bridge Jn.–Brighton	0305 from Manchester P.
	0952		Brighton–Willesden WL Jn.	
	1330		Mitre Bridge Jn.–Dover W.D.	1030 from Liverpool L.S.
	1750		Dover W.D.–Willesden WL Jn.	
47.536:	0550		Paddington–Liverpool L.S.	
	1410	SX	Liverpool L.S.–Reading G.	
	1932	SX	Reading G.–Birmingham N.S.	1732 from Poole.
47.537:	1215	SX	Birmingham N.S.–Penzance	0720 from Glasgow C.
	2135	SX	Penzance–Plymouth	
47.538:	0610		Plymouth–Penzance	2359 from Paddington.
	1027		Penzance–Plymouth	
	1550	SX	Newton Abbot–Exeter St. D.	
	1725	SX	Exeter St. D.–Paignton	
	1838	SX	Paignton–Birmingham N.S.	
	1840	SO	Plymouth–Birmingham N.S.	
47.539:	0656		Birmingham N.S.–Plymouth	2350 from Glasgow C.
	1245		Plymouth–Birmingham N.S.	1027 from Penzance.
	2117	SX	Birmingham N.S.–Paddington	1920 from Manchester P.
47.540:	0604	SX	Hereford–Paddington	
	1702	SX	Paddington–Hereford	
47.541:	0703		Paddington–Manchester P.	
	1401		Manchester P.–Stafford	
	1609		Stafford–Paddington	

47.542:	0904		Canterbury E.–Willesden WL Jn.
	1836	SX	Willesden 58 Signal–Stratford (London)D.86.117
	1838	SO	Willesden 58 Signal–Stratford (London)D.86.117
47.543:	2359	SUN	Paddington–Plymouth
	2359	SX	Paddington–Plymouth
	1028	SX	Plymouth–Birmingham N.S.
	1755	SX	Wolverhampton–Shrewsbury 1540 from Euston.
	2250	SX	Shrewsbury–York
47.544:	2225	SX	York–Shrewsbury
47.545:	0925		Shrewsbury–Wolverhampton 0714 from Aberystwyth.
	1210	SX	Birmingham N.S.–Poole 0745 from Newcastle.
	1732	SX	Poole–Reading G.
	1952	SO	Wolverhampton–Shrewsbury 1740 from Euston.
47.546:	1542	FO	Paddington–Plymouth
47.547:	1905	FO	Paddington–Plymouth
47.548:	1441	FO	Paddington–Plymouth
47.549:	1807	FO	Paddington–Swansea
47.550:	0124		Bristol T.M.–Swansea
	0745		Swansea–Manchester P.
	1412		Manchester P.–Cardiff C.
	2002	SX	Cardiff C.–Crewe
47.551:	0204	MO	Crewe–Cardiff C. 0042 from Manchester P.
	0204	MX	Crewe–Cardiff C.
	0800		Cardiff C.–Bristol T.M.
47.552:	0720		Bristol T.M.–Swansea
	2002	SO	Cardiff C.–Crewe
	2146	SX	Swansea–Bristol T.M. 2044 from Carmarthen.
47.553:	1648	FSX	Bristol T.M.–Weston Super Mare
	1750	FSX	Weston Super Mare–Bristol T.M.
47.554:	2044	SX	Carmarthen–Swansea
47.555:	0550	SX	Cardiff C.–Bristol T.M.
	1008	SX	Bristol T.M.–Portsmouth Hbr.
	1410	SX	Portsmouth Hbr.–Bristol T.M.
47.556:	0630		Cardiff C.–Bristol T.M.
	0859	SO	Bristol T.M.–Cardiff C. 0550 from Portsmouth Hbr.
	1010	SO	Cardiff C.–Bristol T.M.
	1200	SO	Bristol T.M.–Cardiff C. 0830 from Brighton.
	1400	SO	Cardiff C.–Bristol T.M.
47.557:	1200	FO	Bristol T.M.–Cardiff C. 0830 from Brighton.
	1400	FO	Cardiff C.–Bristol T.M.
47.558:	0515		Holyhead–Crewe
	0953		Crewe–Cardiff C. 0714 from Holyhead.
	1535		Cardiff C.–Crewe
	2109		Crewe–Cardiff C.
47.559:	0607		Cardiff C.–Crewe
	1135		Crewe–Cardiff C.
	1735		Cardiff C.–Holyhead
47.560:	1210	SO	Birmingham N.S.–Poole 0745 from Newcastle.
	1732	SO	Poole–Reading G.
47.561:	0808	SO	Hereford–Paddington
	1752	SO	Paddington–Birmingham N.S.
47.562:	2150	SO	Plymouth–Paddington 1920 from Penzance.
47.563:	0950	SO	Swansea–Bristol T.M.
	1250	SO	Bristol T.M.–Swansea 1010 from Portsmouth Hbr.
	1605	SO	Swansea–Bristol T.M.
	1853	SO	Bristol T.M.–Cardiff C. 1610 from Portsmouth Hbr.
47.564:	1354	SO	Bristol T.M.–Cardiff C. 1110 from Portsmouth Hbr.
	1510	SO	Cardiff C.–Bristol T.M.

47.565:	0740	SO	Newton Abbot–Paignton	
	0817	SO	Paignton–Exeter St. D.	
	1105	SO	Exeter St. D.–Brighton	
47.566:	0944	SUN	Mitre Bridge Jn.–Brighton	0700 from Wolverhampton.
	1723	SUN	Brighton–Willesden WL Jn.	
	1914	SUN	Mitre Bridge Jn.–Brighton	1539 from Manchester P.
47.567:	1053	SUN	Brighton–Willesden WL Jn.	
47.568:	0855*	SUN	Liverpool L.S.–Southampton C.	
	0910*	SUN	Liverpool L.S.–Southampton C.	
	1816	SUN	Southampton C.–Reading G.	
47.569:	0730	SUN	Manchester P.–Reading G.	
	1931	SUN	Reading G.–Birmingham N.S.	1816 from Southampton C.
47.570:	1605	SUN	Birmingham N.S.–Penzance	1300 from Manchester P.
47.571:	0745*	SUN	Birmingham N.S.–Bristol T.M.	2310 from Glasgow C.
	0745*	SUN	Birmingham N.S.–Bristol T.M.	2350 from Glasgow C.
	2125	SUN	Bristol T.M.–Birmingham N.S.	
47.572:	1252	SUN	Reading G.–Southampton C.	0730 from Manchester P.
	1548	SUN	Southampton C.–Birmingham N.S.	
	2120	SUN	Birmingham N.S.–Paddington	1920 from Liverpool L.S.
47.573:	1825	SUN	Paddington–Hereford	
47.574:	1317	SUN	York–Weston Super Mare	
	2040	SUN	Weston Super Mare–Paddington	
47.575:	1033	SUN	Kensington O.–Dover W.D.	
	1345	SUN	Dover W.D.–Willesden WL Jn.	
47.576:	2022	SUN	Paddington–Wolverhampton	
47.577:	1405*	SUN	Liverpool L.S.–Paddington	
	1417*	SUN	Liverpool L.S.–Paddington	
47.578:	1730	SUN	Plymouth–Paddington	
47.579:	1830	SUN	Plymouth–Paddington	
47.580:	1640*	SUN	Swansea–Paddington	
47.581:	1245*	SUN	Swansea–Paddington	
47.582:	0131+	SUN	Crewe–Warrington BQ	+1/11–27/12 D.87.029
	0359+	SUN	Warrington BQ–Crewe	+1/11–27/12 D.86.444
	1347+	SUN	Crewe–Warrington BQ	+1/11–27/12 D.87.043
47.583:	1350	SUN	Cardiff C.–Manchester P.	
	1827	SUN	Manchester P.–Cardiff C.	
47.584:	1410	SUN	Holyhead–Cardiff C.	
47.585:	1635	SUN	Cardiff C.–Holyhead	
47.586:	1712	SUN	Brighton–Exeter St. D.	

EASTFIELD DEPOT

47.587:	0529		Carstairs–Perth	
	1333	SO	Glasgow Q.S.–Inverness	
	1714	SX	Glasgow Q.S.–Edinburgh	
	1930	SO	Inverness–Carlisle	
	1955	SX	Edinburgh–Aberdeen	
47.588:	0730	SX	Aberdeen–Carstairs	
	1346	SX	Carstairs–Edinburgh	
	1555	SX	Edinburgh–Inverness	0855 from Euston.
	2100	SX	Inverness–Mossend Yard	
47.589:	0700	SX	Dundee–Carstairs	
	1149	SX	Carstairs–Edinburgh	
	1438	SX	Edinburgh–Carstairs	1030 from Inverness.
	1609	SX	Carstairs–Edinburgh	
	1755	SX	Edinburgh–Dunbar	
	1848	SX	Dunbar–Edinburgh	
	2344	SX	Edinburgh–Carstairs	

47.590:	0428	SX	Mossend Yard–Inverness	2230 from Euston.
	1032	SX	Inverness–Aberdeen	
	1540	SX	Aberdeen–Inverness	
	1930	SX	Inverness–Mossend Yard	
47.591:	0202		Carlisle–Stranraer Hbr.	2105 from Euston.
	1055		Stranraer Hbr.–Carlisle	
47.592:	1352		Carlisle–Glasgow C.	
	1730	SX	Glasgow C.–Carlisle	
	2330	SO	Glasgow Q.S.–Perth	
47.593:	0555		Carlisle–Glasgow C.	
	1013		Glasgow C.–Carlisle	
	1430		Carlisle–Stranraer Hbr.	1000 from Euston.
	2240	SX	Stranraer Hbr.–Carlisle	
47.594:	0748		Carlisle–Glasgow C.	
	1345		Glasgow C.–Carlisle	
	1755		Carlisle–Glasgow C.	
	2215		Glasgow C.–Carlisle	
47.595:	0322	SO	Mossend Yard–Inverness	
	0327	SX	Mossend Yard–Inverness	
	1030		Inverness–Edinburgh	
	1544	SX	Edinburgh–Carstairs	
	1555	SO	Edinburgh–Inverness	0840 from Euston.
	1717	SX	Carstairs–Edinburgh	
47.596:	1223	SO	Glasgow C.–Stranraer Hbr.	
	1835	SO	Stranraer Hbr.–Glasgow C.	
47.597:	1730	SO	Glasgow C.–Carlisle	
47.598:	2215	SUN	Glasgow C.–Carlisle	
47.599:	2100	SUN	Inverness–Mossend Yard	
47.600:	0217	SUN	Carlisle–Inverness	2055 from Euston.
	1930	SUN	Inverness–Mossend Yard	
47.601:	0120	SUN	Perth–Aberdeen	
	1030	SUN	Aberdeen–Edinburgh	
	1614	SUN	Edinburgh–Carstairs	T.47.519
	1832	SUN	Carstairs–Edinburgh	
	2125	SUN	Edinburgh–Aberdeen	
47.602:	1150	SUN	Glasgow C.–Edinburgh	
	1714	SUN	Edinburgh–Carstairs	
	2033	SUN	Carstairs–Edinburgh	
	2344	SUN	Edinburgh–Carstairs	
47.603:	1445	SUN	Glasgow C.–Carlisle	
	1935	SUN	Carlisle–Glasgow C.	

DMU REPLACEMENT DIAGRAMS

The following diagrams operate until further notice vice Sprinter/Pacer units. (Subject to cancellation or alteration at short notice). It should be noted that these three diagrams may be a class 31/4s rather than class 47s.

47.640:	0718		Nottingham–Blackpool N.
	1120		Blackpool N.–Nottingham
47.641:	1544		Nottingham–Blackpool N.
	1944		Blackpool N.–Nottingham
47.642:	0600	SX	Skipton–Carlisle
	0604	SO	Leeds–Carlisle
	1005		Carlisle–Leeds
	1321		Leeds–Carlisle
	1745		Carlisle–Leeds

EXTENDED RANGE LOCOMOTIVES

47.650:	1427		Edinburgh–Aberdeen
	1710		Aberdeen–Huntly
	1820		Huntly–Aberdeen
	2115	SX	Aberdeen–King's Cross
47.651:	1033	SX	King's Cross–Hull
	1505	SX	Hull–King's Cross
47.652:	1910	FO	King's Cross–Newcastle
47.653:	2359	SX	King's Cross–Edinburgh
	2359	SUN	King's Cross–Edinburgh
	1030		Edinburgh–Aberdeen
	1405	SO	Aberdeen–Edinburgh
	1445	SX	Aberdeen–Edinburgh
47.654:	1040		Aberdeen–Edinburgh
	2010	SX	Edinburgh–Newcastle
47.655:	0745	SX	Newcastle–Birmingham N.S.
	1455	SX	Birmingham N.S.–Newcastle
	2300	SX	Newcastle–King's Cross
47.656:	2038	7	King's Cross–Aberdeen
47.657:	0940		Aberdeen–Inverness
	1232		Inverness–Aberdeen
	1625	SX	Aberdeen–Dyce
	1727	SX	Dyce–Montrose
	1837	SX	Montrose–Aberdeen
	2000	SX	Aberdeen–King's Cross
	2025	SO	Aberdeen–King's Cross
47.658:	2215	SX	King's Cross–Aberdeen
47.659:	2215	SUN	King's Cross–Aberdeen
47.660:	1537	SUN	Glasgow C.–Stranraer Hbr.
	1835	SUN	Stranraer Hbr.–Glasgow C.
47.661:	2115	SUN	Aberdeen–King's Cross
47.662:	1110	SUN	King's Cross–Leeds
	1545	SUN	Leeds–King's Cross
47.663:	2000	SUN	Aberdeen–King's Cross
47.664:	2010	SUN	Edinburgh–Newcastle
47.665:	1140	SUN	Edinburgh–York
	2300	SUN	Newcastle–King's Cross
47.666:	1210	SUN	King's Cross–Leeds
	1648	SUN	Leeds–King's Cross

1038 from Poole.
2010 from Edinburgh.

0950 from Glasgow C.
2010 from Edinburgh.

CLASS 47/7

These locomotives are now virtually confined to Scotland all booked workings are north of the border and all major maintenance is now to be carried out at Springburn depot.

47.701:	0708	SX	Dunblane–Edinburgh
	0830		Edinburgh–Glasgow Q.S.
	0930		Glasgow Q.S.–Edinburgh
	1030		Edinburgh–Glasgow Q.S.
	1130		Glasgow Q.S.–Edinburgh
	1230		Edinburgh–Glasgow Q.S.
	1330		Glasgow Q.S.–Edinburgh
	1500		Edinburgh–Glasgow Q.S.
	1600		Glasgow Q.S.–Edinburgh
	1700		Edinburgh–Glasgow Q.S.
	1800		Glasgow Q.S.–Edinburgh
	1900		Edinburgh–Glasgow Q.S.
	2000		Glasgow Q.S.–Edinburgh
	2100		Edinburgh–Glasgow Q.S.
	2200		Glasgow Q.S.–Edinburgh
	2300		Edinburgh–Glasgow Q.S.

47.702:	0730		Edinburgh–Glasgow Q.S.
	0830		Glasgow Q.S.–Edinburgh
	0930		Edinburgh–Glasgow Q.S.
	1030		Glasgow Q.S.–Edinburgh
	1130		Edinburgh–Glasgow Q.S.
	1230		Glasgow Q.S.–Edinburgh
	1400		Edinburgh–Glasgow Q.S.
	1525		Glasgow Q.S.–Dyce
	1845		Dyce–Glasgow Q.S.
	2330	SX	Glasgow Q.S.–Perth
47.703:	0700		Edinburgh–Glasgow Q.S.
	0800		Glasgow Q.S.–Edinburgh
	0900		Edinburgh–Glasgow Q.S.
	1000		Glasgow Q.S.–Edinburgh
	1100		Edinburgh–Glasgow Q.S.
	1200		Glasgow Q.S.–Edinburgh
	1300		Edinburgh–Glasgow Q.S.
	1400		Glasgow Q.S.–Edinburgh
	1600		Edinburgh–Glasgow Q.S.
	1700		Glasgow Q.S.–Edinburgh
	1800		Edinburgh–Glasgow Q.S.
	1900		Glasgow Q.S.–Edinburgh
	2000		Edinburgh–Glasgow Q.S.
	2100		Glasgow Q.S.–Edinburgh
	2200	SO	Edinburgh–Glasgow Q.S.
	2230	SX	Edinburgh–Glasgow Q.S.
	2300	SO	Glasgow Q.S.–Edinburgh
47.704:	0655		Glasgow Q.S.–Edinburgh
	0800		Edinburgh–Glasgow Q.S.
	0900		Glasgow Q.S.–Edinburgh
	1000		Edinburgh–Glasgow Q.S.
	1100		Glasgow Q.S.–Edinburgh
	1200		Edinburgh–Glasgow Q.S.
	1300		Glasgow Q.S.–Edinburgh
	1430		Edinburgh–Glasgow Q.S.
	1530		Glasgow Q.S.–Edinburgh
	1630		Edinburgh–Glasgow Q.S.
	1730		Glasgow Q.S.–Edinburgh
	1830		Edinburgh–Glasgow Q.S.
	1930		Glasgow Q.S.–Edinburgh
	2030		Edinburgh–Glasgow Q.S.
	2130		Glasgow Q.S.–Edinburgh
	2230	SO	Edinburgh–Glasgow Q.S.
47.705:	0725	SX	Glasgow Q.S.–Aberdeen
	0725	SO	Glasgow Q.S.–Aberdeen
	1105		Aberdeen–Glasgow Q.S.
	1430		Glasgow Q.S.–Edinburgh
	1530		Edinburgh–Glasgow Q.S.
	1630		Glasgow Q.S.–Edinburgh
	1730		Edinburgh–Glasgow Q.S.
	1830		Glasgow Q.S.–Edinburgh
	1930		Edinburgh–Glasgow Q.S.
	2030		Glasgow Q.S.–Edinburgh
	2130		Edinburgh–Glasgow Q.S.
	2230		Glasgow Q.S.–Edinburgh
47.706:	0615	SX	Edinburgh–Kirkcaldy
	0730	SX	Kirkcaldy–Edinburgh
	0830		Edinburgh–Aberdeen
	1305		Aberdeen–Glasgow Q.S.
	1725		Glasgow Q.S.–Aberdeen
	2235	SX	Aberdeen–Perth

47.707:	0525	SX	Aberdeen–Glasgow Q.S.
	0525	SO	Aberdeen–Glasgow Q.S.
	0925		Glasgow Q.S.–Aberdeen
	1240		Aberdeen–Edinburgh
	1655		Edinburgh–Aberdeen
	2030		Aberdeen–Edinburgh
47.708:	0110		Perth–Aberdeen
	0700		Aberdeen–Glasgow Q.S.
	1125		Glasgow Q.S.–Aberdeen
	1505		Aberdeen–Glasgow Q.S.
	1925		Glasgow Q.S.–Aberdeen
47.709:	0625		Perth–Dyce
	0845		Dyce–Glasgow Q.S.
	1325		Glasgow Q.S.–Aberdeen
	1705		Aberdeen–Glasgow Q.S.
	2025		Glasgow Q.S.–Dundee
47.710:	0710		Perth–Edinburgh
	1330		Edinburgh–Glasgow Q.S.
	1500		Glasgow Q.S.–Edinburgh
	1713		Edinburgh–Dundee
47.711:	0925	SUN	Glasgow Q.S.–Aberdeen
	1500	SUN	Aberdeen–Glasgow Q.S.
	2330	SUN	Glasgow Q.S.–Perth
47.712:	1100	SUN	Aberdeen–Glasgow Q.S.
	1925	SUN	Glasgow Q.S.–Aberdeen
47.713:	0825	SUN	Dundee–Glasgow Q.S.
	1125	SUN	Glasgow Q.S.–Aberdeen
	1700	SUN	Aberdeen–Glasgow Q.S.
	2125	SUN	Glasgow Q.S.–Dundee
47.714:	1300	SUN	Aberdeen–Glasgow Q.S.
	1725	SUN	Glasgow Q.S.–Aberdeen
	2235	SUN	Aberdeen–Perth
47.715:	1030	SUN	Edinburgh–Aberdeen
	1530	SUN	Aberdeen–Edinburgh
47.716:	1525	SUN	Glasgow Q.S.–Aberdeen
	1900	SUN	Aberdeen–Glasgow Q.S.
47.717:	0800	SUN	Glasgow Q.S.–Edinburgh
	0930	SUN	Edinburgh–Glasgow Q.S.
	1100	SUN	Glasgow Q.S.–Edinburgh
	1230	SUN	Edinburgh–Glasgow Q.S.
	1400	SUN	Glasgow Q.S.–Edinburgh
	1530	SUN	Edinburgh–Glasgow Q.S.
	1700	SUN	Glasgow Q.S.–Edinburgh
	1800	SUN	Edinburgh–Glasgow Q.S.
	1900	SUN	Glasgow Q.S.–Edinburgh
	2000	SUN	Edinburgh–Glasgow Q.S.
	2100	SUN	Glasgow Q.S.–Edinburgh
47.718:	1830	SUN	Edinburgh–Glasgow Q.S.
	1930	SUN	Glasgow Q.S.–Edinburgh
	2030	SUN	Edinburgh–Glasgow Q.S.
	2130	SUN	Glasgow Q.S.–Edinburgh
47.719:	1130	SUN	Edinburgh–Glasgow Q.S.
	1300	SUN	Glasgow Q.S.–Edinburgh
	1430	SUN	Edinburgh–Glasgow Q.S.
	1600	SUN	Glasgow Q.S.–Edinburgh
	1730	SUN	Edinburgh–Glasgow Q.S.
	1830	SUN	Glasgow Q.S.–Edinburgh
	1930	SUN	Edinburgh–Glasgow Q.S.
	2030	SUN	Glasgow Q.S.–Edinburgh
	2130	SUN	Edinburgh–Glasgow Q.S.

47.720: 0900 SUN Glasgow Q.S.–Edinburgh
       1030 SUN Edinburgh–Glasgow Q.S.
       1200 SUN Glasgow Q.S.–Edinburgh
       1330 SUN Edinburgh–Glasgow Q.S.
       1500 SUN Glasgow Q.S.–Edinburgh
       1630 SUN Edinburgh–Glasgow Q.S.
       1800 SUN Glasgow Q.S.–Edinburgh
       1900 SUN Edinburgh–Glasgow Q.S.
       2000 SUN Glasgow Q.S.–Edinburgh
       2100 SUN Edinburgh–Glasgow Q.S.
       2200 SUN Glasgow Q.S.–Edinburgh
       2300 SUN Edinburgh–Glasgow Q.S.

CLASS 47/9

The sole member of this sub class is confined to freight work on the Western Region and is not expected to appear on passenger work other than following failures.

CLASS 50/0

The workings for this sub class remain largely unchanged from recent years.

50.001: 0820 SX Paddington–Oxford
        0955 SX Oxford–Paddington
        1754 SX Paddington–Twyford
50.002: 0654 SX Oxford–Paddington
        1730 SX Paddington–Oxford
        1912 SX Oxford–Paddington
50.003: 0750 SX Oxford–Paddington
        1705 SX Paddington–Didcot Parkway
        2022 SX Paddington–Oxford
50.004: 0640 SX Oxford–Paddington
        1055 SO Oxford–Paddington
        1317   Paddington–Oxford
        1600 SO Oxford–Paddington
        1752 SX Paddington–Wolverhampton
        2022 SO Paddington–Oxford
        2235 SX Wolverhampton–Oxford
50.005: 0743 SX Twyford–Paddington
        1055 SX Oxford–Paddington
        1832 SX Paddington–Oxford
        2012 SX Oxford–Paddington
50.006: 0706 SX Newbury–Paddington
        1816 SX Paddington–Twyford
50.007: 0707 SX Banbury–Paddington
        1814 SX Paddington–Oxford
50.008: 0628 SX Oxford–Paddington
        1300   Oxford–Paddington
        1517   Paddington–Oxford
        1655 SX Oxford–Paddington
        1655 SO Oxford–Paddington
        1922 SX Paddington–Reading G.
50.009: 0647 SX Westbury–Paddington
        1727 SX Paddington–Westbury
        2310 FO Bristol T.M.–Swindon
50.010: 0651 SX Leamington Spa–Paddington
        1217   Paddington–Oxford
        1355   Oxford–Paddington
        1612 SX Paddington–Oxford
        1617 SO Paddington–Oxford
        1740 SX Oxford–Paddington
        1912 SO Oxford–Paddington
        2045 SO Paddington–Exeter St. D.

```
50.011: 0600  SX   Reading G.–Oxford
        0713  SX   Oxford–Paddington
        1200       Oxford–Paddington
        1417       Paddington–Oxford
        1600  SX   Oxford–Paddington
        1753  SX   Paddington–Banbury
50.012: 0735  SO   Oxford–Paddington
        0921  SX   Didcot Parkway–Paddington
        1117       Paddington–Birmingham N.S.
        1440  SX   Birmingham N.S.–Paddington
        1440  SO   Birmingham N.S.–Paddington
        1909  SX   Paddington–Oxford
50.013: 0726  SX   Oxford–Paddington
        0917       Paddington–Birmingham N.S.
        1310  SX   Birmingham N.S.–Paddington
        1310  SO   Birmingham N.S.–Paddington
        1705  SO   Paddington–Oxford
        1810  SX   Paddington–Newbury
        2012  SO   Oxford–Paddington
50.014: 0740  SX   Newton Abbot–Paignton
        0817  SX   Paignton–Exeter St. D.
        1105  SX   Exeter St. D.–Portsmouth Hbr.
        1530  SX   Portsmouth Hbr.–Waterloo
        1910  SX   Waterloo–Exeter St. D.
50.015: 0140  SO   Waterloo–Yeovil Jn.
        0510  SO   Yeovil Jn.–Salisbury
        0550  SX   Exeter St. D.–Waterloo
        0700  SO   Salisbury–Waterloo
        1110       Waterloo–Exeter St. D.
        1618       Exeter St. D.–Waterloo
        2210       Waterloo–Salisbury
50.016: 0138  MX   Eastleigh–Waterloo            2238 from Weymouth.
        0910       Waterloo–Exeter St. D.
        1417       Exeter St. D.–Waterloo
        2038       Waterloo–Yeovil Jn.
50.017: 0609  SX   Salisbury–Exeter St. D.
        0938  SX   Exeter St. D.–Waterloo
        1642  SX   Waterloo–Exeter St. D.
50.018: 0642       Exeter St. D.–Waterloo
        1310       Waterloo–Exeter St. D.
        1733  SX   Exeter St. D.–Waterloo
        1817  SO   Exeter St. D.–Waterloo
50.019: 0140  SX   Waterloo–Yeovil Jn.
        0515  SX   Yeovil Jn.–Salisbury
        0640  SX   Salisbury–Waterloo
        0925  SX   Waterloo–Portsmouth Hbr.
        1203  SX   Portsmouth Hbr.–Paignton
        1640  SX   Paignton–Exeter St. D.
50.020: 0640       Totnes–Exeter St. D.
        0811  SX   Exeter St. D.–Waterloo
        0817  SO   Exeter St. D.–Waterloo
        1510       Waterloo–Exeter St. D.
        1947  SX   Exeter St. D.–Waterloo
50.021: 0700       Waterloo–Exeter St. D.
        1218       Exeter St. D.–Waterloo
        1738  SX   Waterloo–Exeter St. D.
        1910  SO   Waterloo–Exeter St. D.
        2151       Exeter St. D.–Newton Abbot
50.022: 0635  SO   Bristol T.M.–Plymouth
        1557       Plymouth–Penzance
        1830  SO   Penzance–Plymouth
```

50.023:	0624	SX	Newton Abbot–Exeter St. D.
	0750		Exeter St. D.–Paignton
	0855		Paignton–Newton Abbot
	0940		Newton Abbot–Paignton
	1025		Paignton–Exeter St. D.
	1325		Exeter St. D.–Paignton
	1430		Paignton–Newton Abbot
	1713		Bristol T.M.–Taunton
	1900		Taunton–Bristol T.M.
	2235	SX	Bristol T.M.–Exeter St. D.
50.024:	0702		Exeter St. D.–Penzance
	1214		Penzance–Plymouth	2 x 50 SO
	1520	FSX	Plymouth–Penzance
	1621	SO	Plymouth–Bristol T.M.	2 x 50
	1830	SX	Penzance–Plymouth
	2320*	SO	Bristol T.M.–Cardiff C.	2025 from Portsmouth Hbr.
50.025:	1525	SX	Penzance–Plymouth
50.026:	0635	SX	Bristol T.M.–Plymouth
	1621	SX	Plymouth–Bristol T.M.
	2008	SX	Bristol T.M.–Cardiff C.	1710 from Portsmouth Hbr.
50.027:	0726		Swindon–Taunton
	1000		Taunton–Bristol T.M.
	1648	SO	Bristol T.M.–Weston Super Mare
	1750	SO	Weston Super Mare–Bristol T.M.
50.028:	0645		Swindon–Penzance
	1640	SO	Plymouth–Penzance	0720 from Glasgow C.
	2100	SX	Plymouth–Bristol T.M.	1830 from Penzance.
50.029:	0911	SX	Penzance–Plymouth
	1437	FO	Plymouth–Paddington
	1902	FO	Paddington–Bristol T.M.
50.030:	0817	SO	Paddington–Oxford
	0955	SO	Oxford–Paddington
	1909	SO	Paddington–Oxford
	2108	SO	Oxford–Paddington
	2335	SO	Paddington–Westbury
50.031:	0602	SO	Salisbury–Exeter St. D.
	0936	SO	Exeter St. D.–Waterloo
	1710	SO	Waterloo–Exeter St. D.
	2151	SO	Exeter St. D.–Newton Abbot
50.032:	0911	SO	Penzance–Plymouth
	1520	SO	Plymouth–Penzance
	1920	SO	Penzance–Plymouth
50.033:	2325	SO	Paddington–Penzance	T.50.054
50.034:	1530	SO	Exeter St. D.–Paignton	1112 from Brighton.
	1640	SO	Paignton–Exeter St. D.
	2025	SO	Exeter St. D.–Basingstoke
50.035:	1812	SO	Paddington–Hereford
50.036:	0845	SUN	Exeter St. D.–Paddington
	2130	SUN	Oxford–Paddington
50.037:	1100	SUN	Paddington–Oxford
	1325	SUN	Oxford–Paddington
50.038:	1115	SUN	Oxford–Paddington
	1400	SUN	Paddington–Hereford
	1825	SUN	Hereford–Paddington
50.039:	1110*	SUN	Waterloo–Exeter St. D.
	1110*	SUN	Waterloo–Honiton
	1555*	SUN	Exeter St. D.–Waterloo
	1607*	SUN	Exeter St. D.–Waterloo
	1619*	SUN	Honiton–Waterloo
	2110+	SUN	Waterloo–Yeovil Jn.	+ Not 7/2–20/3
	2210+	SUN	Waterloo–Salisbury	+ 7/2–20/3

```
50.040:  0925* SUN  Exeter St. D.–Waterloo
         0949* SUN  Honiton–Waterloo
         1710  SUN  Waterloo–Exeter St. D.
         2105  SUN  Exeter St. D.–Salisbury
50.041:  0910* SUN  Waterloo–Exeter St. D.
         0910* SUN  Waterloo–Honiton
         1420* SUN  Exeter St. D.–Waterloo
         1446* SUN  Honiton–Waterloo
         2010  SUN  Waterloo–Exeter St. D.
50.042:  1620  SUN  Plymouth–Waterloo           1410 from Penzance.
50.043:  0130* SUN  Waterloo–Salisbury
         0130* SUN  Waterloo–Salisbury
         0825  SUN  Salisbury–Waterloo
         1410  SUN  Waterloo–Exeter St. D.
50.044:  0826* SUN  Basingstoke–Exeter St. D.
         0826* SUN  Basingstoke–Honiton
         1225* SUN  Exeter St. D.–Waterloo
         1249* SUN  Honiton–Waterloo
         1910  SUN  Waterloo–Exeter St. D.
50.045:  1615  SUN  Hereford–Paddington
50.046:  1200  SUN  Paddington–Oxford
50.047:  0955  SUN  Oxford–Paddington
50.048:  1610  SUN  Paddington–Oxford
50.049:  0845* SUN  Oxford–Paddington
         0902* SUN  Didcot Parkway–Paddington
         1720  SUN  Oxford–Paddington
50.050:  1930  SUN  Bristol T.M.–Paddington     2 x 50
50.051:  1725* SUN  Exeter St. D.–Waterloo
         1745* SUN  Exeter St. D.–Waterloo
50.052:  1825  SUN  Exeter St. D.–Waterloo
50.053:  1650  SUN  Paddington–Bristol T.M.
50.054:  0317* SUN  Newton Abbot–Plymouth       T.50.033
         0334* SUN  Newton Abbot–Plymouth       T.50.033
         0351* SUN  Newton Abbot–Plymouth       T.50.033
50.055:  1425  SUN  Plymouth–Birmingham N.S.
         2036  SUN  Birmingham N.S.–Plymouth    1030 from Aberdeen.
50.056:  1040  SUN  Penzance–Plymouth
50.057:  2140  SUN  Penzance–Plymouth
```

CLASS 50/1

The sole member of this sub class is confined to freight work on the Western Region and is not expected to appear on passenger work other than following failures.

CLASSES 56 & 58

Both these classes are designed for exclusive use by the freight sector, but have seen passenger work in the past following failures and at times of emergency and locomotive shortage. They also have appeared from time to time on railtours, but the most regular workings have been on the West Coast Main Line and branches on Sundays when overhead line equipment has been isolated necessitating diesel haulage of normally electrically hauled trains through the isolated sections. Although it is possible that this use may continue in the future, the increased sectorisation of BRs business activities makes such use of these locomotives less likely than in the past. In addition, class 56 locomotives fresh from classified repair or F exam at BREL Crewe Works may be used as pilot locomotives on trains between Crewe and Holyhead from time to time for test purposes.

CLASS 59

By nature of the fact that these locomotives are privately owned by Foster Yeoman, use on passenger trains is not expected except in an emergency to clear a failure from the running line.

CLASS 73

Workings are broadly similar to recent years. Other than the Gatwick–Victoria workings shown below, most workings may be performed by either class 73/0 or 73/1 subject to suitable manning arrangements being made.

73.101:	0530	7	Victoria–Gatwick Airport
	0620	7	Gatwick Airport–Victoria
	0715	7	Victoria–Gatwick Airport
	0805	7	Gatwick Airport–Victoria
	0900	7	Victoria–Gatwick Airport
	0950	7	Gatwick Airport–Victoria
	1045	7	Victoria–Gatwick Airport
	1135	7	Gatwick Airport–Victoria
	1230	7	Victoria–Gatwick Airport
	1320	7	Gatwick Airport–Victoria
	1415	7	Victoria–Gatwick Airport
	1505	7	Gatwick Airport–Victoria
	1600	7	Victoria–Gatwick Airport
	1650	7	Gatwick Airport–Victoria
	1745	7	Victoria–Gatwick Airport
	1835	7	Gatwick Airport–Victoria
	1930	7	Victoria–Gatwick Airport
	2020	7	Gatwick Airport–Victoria
	2115	7	Victoria–Gatwick Airport
	2205	7	Gatwick Airport–Victoria
	2300	7	Victoria–Gatwick Airport
	2350	7	Gatwick Airport–Victoria
73.102:	0545	7	Victoria–Gatwick Airport
	0635	7	Gatwick Airport–Victoria
	0730	7	Victoria–Gatwick Airport
	0820	7	Gatwick Airport–Victoria
	0915	7	Victoria–Gatwick Airport
	1005	7	Gatwick Airport–Victoria
	1100	7	Victoria–Gatwick Airport
	1150	7	Gatwick Airport–Victoria
	1245	7	Victoria–Gatwick Airport
	1335	7	Gatwick Airport–Victoria
	1430	7	Victoria–Gatwick Airport
	1520	7	Gatwick Airport–Victoria
	1615	7	Victoria–Gatwick Airport
	1705	7	Gatwick Airport–Victoria
	1800	7	Victoria–Gatwick Airport
	1850	7	Gatwick Airport–Victoria
	1945	7	Victoria–Gatwick Airport
	2035	7	Gatwick Airport–Victoria
	2130	7	Victoria–Gatwick Airport
	2220	7	Gatwick Airport–Victoria
	2300	7	Victoria–Gatwick Airport
73.103:	0600	7	Victoria–Gatwick Airport
	0650	7	Gatwick Airport–Victoria
	0745	7	Victoria–Gatwick Airport
	0835	7	Gatwick Airport–Victoria
	0930	7	Victoria–Gatwick Airport
	1020	7	Gatwick Airport–Victoria
	1115	7	Victoria–Gatwick Airport
	1205	7	Gatwick Airport–Victoria
	1300	7	Victoria–Gatwick Airport

	1350	7	Gatwick Airport–Victoria
	1445	7	Victoria–Gatwick Airport
	1535	7	Gatwick Airport–Victoria
	1630	7	Victoria–Gatwick Airport
	1720	7	Gatwick Airport–Victoria
	1815	7	Victoria–Gatwick Airport
	1905	7	Gatwick Airport–Victoria
	2000	7	Victoria–Gatwick Airport
	2050	7	Gatwick Airport–Victoria
	2145	7	Victoria–Gatwick Airport
	2235	7	Gatwick Airport–Victoria
73.104:	0615	7	Victoria–Gatwick Airport
	0705	7	Gatwick Airport–Victoria
	0800	7	Victoria–Gatwick Airport
	0850	7	Gatwick Airport–Victoria
	0945	7	Victoria–Gatwick Airport
	1035	7	Gatwick Airport–Victoria
	1130	7	Victoria–Gatwick Airport
	1220	7	Gatwick Airport–Victoria
	1315	7	Victoria–Gatwick Airport
	1405	7	Gatwick Airport–Victoria
	1500	7	Victoria–Gatwick Airport
	1550	7	Gatwick Airport–Victoria
	1645	7	Victoria–Gatwick Airport
	1735	7	Gatwick Airport–Victoria
	1830	7	Victoria–Gatwick Airport
	1920	7	Gatwick Airport–Victoria
	2015	7	Victoria–Gatwick Airport
	2105	7	Gatwick Airport–Victoria
	2200	7	Victoria–Gatwick Airport
	2320	7	Gatwick Airport–Victoria
	0015	7	Victoria–Gatwick Airport
	0105	7	Gatwick Airport–Victoria
73.105:	0630	7	Victoria–Gatwick Airport
	0720	7	Gatwick Airport–Victoria
	0815	7	Victoria–Gatwick Airport
	0905	7	Gatwick Airport–Victoria
	1000	7	Victoria–Gatwick Airport
	1050	7	Gatwick Airport–Victoria
	1145	7	Victoria–Gatwick Airport
	1235	7	Gatwick Airport–Victoria
	1330	7	Victoria–Gatwick Airport
	1420	7	Gatwick Airport–Victoria
	1515	7	Victoria–Gatwick Airport
	1605	7	Gatwick Airport–Victoria
	1700	7	Victoria–Gatwick Airport
	1750	7	Gatwick Airport–Victoria
	1845	7	Victoria–Gatwick Airport
	1935	7	Gatwick Airport–Victoria
	2030	7	Victoria–Gatwick Airport
	2120	7	Gatwick Airport–Victoria
73.106:	0645	7	Victoria–Gatwick Airport
	0735	7	Gatwick Airport–Victoria
	0830	7	Victoria–Gatwick Airport
	0920	7	Gatwick Airport–Victoria
	1015	7	Victoria–Gatwick Airport
	1105	7	Gatwick Airport–Victoria
	1200	7	Victoria–Gatwick Airport
	1250	7	Gatwick Airport–Victoria
	1345	7	Victoria–Gatwick Airport
	1435	7	Gatwick Airport–Victoria
	1530	7	Victoria–Gatwick Airport
	1620	7	Gatwick Airport–Victoria

	1715	7	Victoria–Gatwick Airport	
	1805	7	Gatwick Airport–Victoria	
	1900	7	Victoria–Gatwick Airport	
	1950	7	Gatwick Airport–Victoria	
	2045	7	Victoria–Gatwick Airport	
	2135	7	Gatwick Airport–Victoria	
	2230	7	Victoria–Gatwick Airport	
	2335		Gatwick Airport–Victoria	
73.107:	0700	7	Victoria–Gatwick Airport	
	0750	7	Gatwick Airport–Victoria	
	0845	7	Victoria–Gatwick Airport	
	0935	7	Gatwick Airport–Victoria	
	1030	7	Victoria–Gatwick Airport	
	1120	7	Gatwick Airport–Victoria	
	1215	7	Victoria–Gatwick Airport	
	1305	7	Gatwick Airport–Victoria	
	1400	7	Victoria–Gatwick Airport	
	1450	7	Gatwick Airport–Victoria	
	1545	7	Victoria–Gatwick Airport	
	1635	7	Gatwick Airport–Victoria	
	1730	7	Victoria–Gatwick Airport	
	1820	7	Gatwick Airport–Victoria	
	1915	7	Victoria–Gatwick Airport	
	2005	7	Gatwick Airport–Victoria	
	2100	7	Victoria–Gatwick Airport	
	2150	7	Gatwick Airport–Victoria	
73.108:	2252	SO	Waterloo–Eastleigh	
73.109:	0744		Waterloo–Bournemouth	
	1100		Bournemouth–Waterloo	
	1344		Waterloo–Bournemouth	
	1700		Bournemouth–Waterloo	
	1944	SX	Waterloo–Bournemouth	
73.110:	0715	SX	Bournemouth–Waterloo	0609 from Weymouth.
	0741	SO	Poole–Waterloo	M.33.108
	1044		Waterloo–Bournemouth	
	1400		Bournemouth–Waterloo	
	1644	SO	Waterloo–Bournemouth	
	1716	SX	Waterloo–Bournemouth	
73.111:	1000		Bournemouth–Waterloo	
	1244		Waterloo–Bournemouth	
	1600		Bournemouth–Waterloo	
	1844		Waterloo–Bournemouth	
	2140	SX	Bournemouth–Waterloo	
73.112:	0900		Bournemouth–Waterloo	
	1144		Waterloo–Bournemouth	
	1500		Bournemouth–Waterloo	
	1744	SO	Waterloo–Bournemouth	
73.113:	0725	SX	Bournemouth–Eastleigh	
73.114:	1544	SX	Waterloo–Bournemouth	
	1900	SX	Bournemouth–Waterloo	
	2144	SX	Waterloo–Bournemouth	
73.115:	0330		London Br.–Dover W.D.	
73.116:	0245		London Br.–Deal	
73.117:	0310		London Br.–Sittingbourne	
73.118:	1744	SUN	Waterloo–Bournemouth	
73.119:	0739	SUN	Poole–Waterloo	M.33.113 or 33.116
	1644	SUN	Waterloo–Bournemouth	
73.120:	0944	SUN	Waterloo–Bournemouth	
	1258	SUN	Bournemouth–Waterloo	1140 from Weymouth.
	1544	SUN	Waterloo–Bournemouth	
	1858	SUN	Bournemouth–Waterloo	

73.121:	1758	SUN	Bournemouth–Waterloo
73.122:	1558+	SUN	Bournemouth–Waterloo
	1830+	SUN	Waterloo–Bournemouth
73.123:	0340	SUN	Waterloo–Petersfield
	0600	SUN	Petersfield–Guildford
	0710	SUN	Guildford–Woking
73.124:	0409	SUN	London Br.–Ramsgate

+ From 20/3
+ From 20/3

CLASS 81

This class is now nominally restricted to 80 mph and as such is not expected to appear on passenger workings except due to shortage of other motive power.

CLASSES 82 & 83

The few surviving members of these classes are exclusively used on ecs duties in the Euston area and are restricted to 40 mph only. As a result, use on passenger trains is unlikely except following failures in the Euston area.

CLASS 85

Many of this class are now also restricted to 80 mph, with a similar note to that for class 81 applying. However, there are two diagrams for the surviving 100 mph locomotives.

| 85.001: | 2338 | SX | Preston–Stafford | 2149 from Barrow in Furness. |
| 85.002: | 1935 | FO | Euston–Liverpool L.S. | |

CLASS 86

This class, along with class 87, forms the staple power for most passenger trains in areas electrified on the overhead system. In the following diagrams, it should be noted that turns 86.1xx may only be worked by class 86/2, but all other turns may be worked by any locomotive of classes 86/1, 86/2 or 86/4. The turns numbered 86.4xx are booked for locomotives fitted with multiple working equipment and hence should currently be worked by class 86/4, although plans to equip class 86/2 have been approved (with a different system) and work has commenced.

EAST ANGLIAN DIAGRAMS

86.101:	0755	SO	Norwich–Liverpool St.	
	0800	SX	Norwich–Liverpool St.	
	1130	SX	Liverpool St.–Norwich	
	1130	SO	Liverpool St.–Norwich	
	1455	SO	Norwich–Liverpool St.	
	1505	SX	Norwich–Liverpool St.	
	1830		Liverpool St.–Norwich	
86.102:	0755	SX	Norwich–Liverpool St.	
	0905	SO	Cambridge–Liverpool St.	0800 from King's Lynn.
	1135		Liverpool St.–Cambridge	
	1305		Cambridge–Liverpool St.	
	1535		Liverpool St.–Cambridge	
	1705		Cambridge–Liverpool St.	
	1935	SO	Liverpool St.–Cambridge	
	2035	MX	Liverpool St.–Cambridge	
	2035	FO	Liverpool St.–Cambridge	
86.103:	0803	SX	Cambridge–Liverpool St.	
	0805	SO	Cambridge–Liverpool St.	0655 from King's Lynn.
	1035		Liverpool St.–Cambridge	
	1205		Cambridge–Liverpool St.	1100 from King's Lynn.
	1435		Liverpool St.–Cambridge	
	1605		Cambridge–Liverpool St.	1500 from King's Lynn.
	1835	SX	Liverpool St.–Cambridge	
	2010	SX	Cambridge–Liverpool St.	1905 from King's Lynn.

86.104:	0835		Liverpool St.–Cambridge
	1005		Cambridge–Liverpool St.	0900 from King's Lynn.
	1235		Liverpool St.–Cambridge
	1405		Cambridge–Liverpool St.	1300 from King's Lynn.
	1620	SX	Liverpool St.–Harwich P.Q.
	1635	SO	Liverpool St.–Cambridge
	1805	SO	Cambridge–Liverpool St.	1700 from King's Lynn.
	1840*	SX	Harwich P.Q.–Liverpool St.
	2035	SO	Liverpool St.–Cambridge
86.105:	0540	SX	Ipswich–Liverpool St.
	0725	SO	Norwich–Liverpool St.
	0830	SX	Liverpool St.–Norwich
	1155	SX	Norwich–Liverpool St.
	1530		Liverpool St.–Norwich
	1855		Norwich–Liverpool St.
86.106:	0618	SX	Norwich–Liverpool St.
	0940		Liverpool St.–Harwich P.Q.
	1635	SX	Liverpool St.–Cambridge
	1840	SX	Cambridge–Liverpool St.	1735 from King's Lynn.
	2135	SX	Liverpool St.–Cambridge
86.107:	0423		Liverpool St.–Cambridge
	0655	SO	Cambridge–Liverpool St.
	0705	SX	Cambridge–Liverpool St.
	0935		Liverpool St.–Cambridge
	1105		Cambridge–Liverpool St.
	1335		Liverpool St.–Cambridge
	1505		Cambridge–Liverpool St.
	1735	SX	Liverpool St.–Cambridge
	1835	SO	Liverpool St.–Cambridge
	2045	SO	Cambridge–Liverpool St.	1940 from King's Lynn.
86.108:	0750	SO	Harwich P.Q.–Liverpool St.
	0855	SX	Cambridge–Liverpool St.	0745 from King's Lynn.
	2030		Liverpool St.–Norwich
86.109:	0540	SX	Norwich–Liverpool St.
	0555	SO	Norwich–Liverpool St.
	0930		Liverpool St.–Norwich
	1255		Norwich–Liverpool St.
	1630		Liverpool St.–Norwich
	2025		Norwich–Liverpool St.
86.110:	1820	FO	Liverpool St.–Norwich
86.111:	0435		Liverpool St.–Ipswich
	0730		Ipswich–Norwich
	0955		Norwich–Liverpool St.
	1330		Liverpool St.–Norwich
	1655		Norwich–Liverpool St.
	1950		Liverpool St.–Harwich P.Q.
86.112:	0745	SX	Harwich P.Q.–Liverpool St.
	1740	SX	Liverpool St.–Norwich
86.113:	0720		Liverpool St.–Norwich
	1055		Norwich–Liverpool St.
	1430		Liverpool St.–Norwich
	1755		Norwich–Liverpool St.
	2130		Liverpool St.–Norwich
86.114:	0655	SO	Norwich–Liverpool St.
	0700	SX	Norwich–Liverpool St.
	1030		Liverpool St.–Norwich
	1355		Norwich–Liverpool St.
	1700	SX	Liverpool St.–Norwich
	1730	SO	Liverpool St.–Norwich

86.115:	0855		Norwich–Liverpool St.
	1230		Liverpool St.–Norwich
	1555		Norwich–Liverpool St.
	1930		Liverpool St.–Norwich
86.116:	0440	SO	Norwich–Liverpool St.
	0830	SO	Liverpool St.–Norwich
	1155	SO	Norwich–Liverpool St.
	1840*	SO	Harwich P.Q.–Liverpool St.
86.117:	1145		Glasgow C.–Harwich P.Q.	P.47.542
86.118:	0750		Harwich P.Q.–Glasgow C.	P.47.533
	1850	SO	Glasgow C.–Preston
	1920	SX	Glasgow C.–Preston
86.119:	0855	SUN	Norwich–Liverpool St.
	1430	SUN	Liverpool St.–Norwich
	1755	SUN	Norwich–Liverpool St.
	2130	SUN	Liverpool St.–Norwich
86.120:	0935	SUN	Liverpool St.–Cambridge
	1215	SUN	Cambridge–Liverpool St.
	1635	SUN	Liverpool St.–Cambridge
	1835	SUN	Cambridge–Liverpool St.	1730 from King's Lynn.
	2305	SUN	Liverpool St.–Cambridge
86.121:	1055	SUN	Norwich–Liverpool St.
	1840*	SUN	Harwich P.Q.–Liverpool St.
86.122:	0550	SUN	Ipswich–Liverpool St.
	0920	SUN	Liverpool St.–Harwich P.Q.
86.123:	1630	SUN	Liverpool St.–Norwich
86.124:	1435	SUN	Liverpool St.–Cambridge
	1615	SUN	Cambridge–Liverpool St.	1500 from King's Lynn.
	2035	SUN	Liverpool St.–Cambridge
86.125:	2030	SUN	Liverpool St.–Norwich
86.126:	1415	SUN	Cambridge–Liverpool St.	1300 from King's Lynn.
	1835	SUN	Liverpool St.–Cambridge
	2055	SUN	Cambridge–Liverpool St.	1950 from King's Lynn.
86.127:	1655	SUN	Norwich–Liverpool St.
	1950	SUN	Liverpool St.–Harwich P.Q.
86.128:	0830	SUN	Liverpool St.–Norwich
	1255	SUN	Norwich–Liverpool St.
	1730	SUN	Liverpool St.–Norwich
	2025	SUN	Norwich–Liverpool St.
86.129:	1855	SUN	Norwich–Liverpool St.
	2300	SUN	Liverpool St.–Norwich
86.130:	0655	SUN	Norwich–Liverpool St.
	1230	SUN	Liverpool St.–Norwich
	1555	SUN	Norwich–Liverpool St.
	1930	SUN	Liverpool St.–Norwich
86.131:	0725	SUN	Harwich P.Q.–Liverpool St.
	1030	SUN	Liverpool St.–Norwich
	1355	SUN	Norwich–Liverpool St.
	1830	SUN	Liverpool St.–Norwich
86.132:	1330	SUN	Harwich P.Q.–Birmingham N.S.	P.47.418
	1818	SUN	Birmingham N.S.–Harwich P.Q.	P.47.418

WEST COAST MAIN LINE DIAGRAMS

86.201:	0015		Liverpool L.S.–Stafford
	0205		Stafford–Manchester P.
	0805	SX	Manchester P.–Euston	T.86.421 MO
	0820	SO	Manchester P.–Euston
	1240	SX	Euston–Wolverhampton
	1340	SO	Euston–Wolverhampton

34

```
        1526  SX   Wolverhampton–Euston
        1726  SO   Wolverhampton–Euston
        1945  SX   Euston–Northampton
86.202: 0625       Liverpool L.S.–Euston
        1140  SO   Euston–Wolverhampton
        1200       Euston–Preston
        1624  SO   Wolverhampton–Euston          1531 from Shrewsbury.
        1709  SX   Preston–Euston                1630 from Blackpool N.
        2028  SO   Euston–Manchester P.
86.203: 0826  SX   Wolverhampton–Euston
        1140  SX   Euston–Wolverhampton
        1624  SX   Wolverhampton–Euston          1531 from Shrewsbury.
        1940  SX   Euston–Wolverhampton
86.204: 0615  SX   Manchester P.–Stafford
        0845       Stafford–Liverpool L.S.
        1130  SX   Liverpool L.S.–Birmingham Int.
        1150  SO   Liverpool L.S.–Euston
        1517  SX   Birmingham Int.–Manchester P.
        1640  SO   Euston–Wolverhampton
        1920  SX   Manchester P.–Birmingham N.S.
        2026  SO   Wolverhampton–Euston
        2210  SX   Birmingham N.S.–Liverpool L.S.  1732 from Poole.
86.205: 0920  SX   Liverpool L.S.–Birmingham N.S.
        1139  SX   Birmingham N.S.–Liverpool L.S.
        1500  SX   Liverpool L.S.–Euston
        2000  SX   Euston–Manchester P.
86.206: 0030       Manchester P.–Euston
        0740  SO   Euston–Wolverhampton
        0840  SX   Euston–Wolverhampton
        1126       Wolverhampton–Euston
        1440  SX   Euston–Wolverhampton
        1600  SO   Euston–Manchester P.
        1726  SX   Wolverhampton–Euston
        2000  SO   Manchester P.–Euston
        2340  SO   Euston–Wolverhampton
86.207: 0705  SX   Manchester P.–Euston
        1130  SX   Euston–Crewe
        1512  SX   Crewe–Euston                  1255 from Holyhead.
        1920  SX   Euston–Liverpool L.S.
86.208: 0710  SX   Euston–Lancaster
        0828  SO   Coventry–Lancaster
        1330       Lancaster–Euston
        1800  SX   Euston–Manchester P.
        1840  SO   Euston–Wolverhampton
86.209: 0950  SX   Liverpool L.S.–Euston
        1714  SX   Euston–Northampton
86.210: 0749  SX   Bletchley–Euston
        0925  SX   Euston–Northampton
        1102  SX   Northampton–Euston
        1310  SX   Euston–Birmingham N.S.
        1518  SX   Birmingham N.S.–Euston
        1840  SX   Euston–Wolverhampton
        2156  FSX  Wolverhampton–Euston
86.211: 0740  SX   Birmingham N.S.–Euston
        1110  SX   Euston–Birmingham N.S.
        1318  SX   Birmingham N.S.–Euston
        1720  SX   Euston–Bletchley
86.212: 0720  SX   Glasgow C.–Birmingham N.S.
        1259  SX   Birmingham N.S.–Glasgow C.    0834 from Poole.
```

86.213:	0740	SX	Euston–Wolverhampton
	1226	SX	Wolverhampton–Euston	1133 from Shrewsbury.
	1640	SX	Euston–Wolverhampton
	2026	SX	Wolverhampton–Euston
	2350	FSX	Euston–Crewe
86.214:	0825	SX	Preston–Glasgow C.	0735 from Manchester V.
	1410	SX	Glasgow C.–Euston
	2050	SX	Euston–Manchester P.
86.215:	0810	SX	Northampton–Euston
	1040	SX	Euston–Wolverhampton
	1326	SX	Wolverhampton–Euston
	1750	SX	Euston–Liverpool L.S.
86.216:	0650		Euston–Manchester P.
	1130	SX	Manchester P.–Euston
	1148	SO	Manchester P.–Euston
	1540	SX	Euston–Wolverhampton
	1550	SO	Euston–Liverpool L.S.
	1926	SX	Birmingham N.S.–Liverpool L.S.	1458 from Poole.
86.217:	0720		Liverpool L.S.–Mitre Bridge Jn.
	1140		Willesden WL Jn.–Liverpool L.S.	0904 from Canterbury E.
	1650	FO	Liverpool L.S.–Euston
	1705	FX	Liverpool L.S.–Euston
	1805	SO	Liverpool L.S.–Euston
	2105	SX	Euston–Carlisle
	2210	SO	Euston–Wolverhampton
86.218:	0659	SX	Preston–Euston	0620 from Blackpool N.
	1150	SX	Euston–Manchester P.
	1630	SX	Manchester P.–Euston
	2030	SX	Euston–Liverpool L.S.
86.219:	0638	SX	Birmingham N.S.–Euston
	0930	SX	Euston–Crewe
	1600	SX	Manchester P.–Euston
	2110	SX	Euston–Wolverhampton
86.220:	1026	SX	Wolverhampton–Euston	0714 from Aberystwyth.
	1617	SX	Euston–Crewe
	1954	SX	Crewe–Birmingham N.S.	1710 from Holyhead.
86.221:	0926	SX	Wolverhampton–Euston
	1745	SX	Euston–Northampton
86.222:	1030		Liverpool L.S.–Mitre Bridge Jn.
	1449		Willesden WL Jn.–Liverpool L.S.	1322 from Brighton.
	1900	SX	Liverpool L.S.–Birmingham N.S.
	1920	SO	Liverpool L.S.–Euston
86.223:	0743	SX	Northampton–Euston
	1410	SX	Euston–Birmingham N.S.
	1618	SX	Birmingham N.S.–Euston
	1930	SX	Euston–Preston
86.224:	0715	SX	Northampton–Euston
	1026	SO	Wolverhampton–Euston	0714 from Aberystwyth.
	1100	SX	Euston–Northampton
	1302	SX	Northampton–Euston
	1630		Euston–Preston
86.225:	0723	SX	Manchester P.–Euston
	1325	SX	Euston–Northampton
	1555	SX	Northampton–Euston
	1810	SX	Euston–Wolverhampton
86.226:	1116		Preston–Glasgow C.	1025 from Manchester V.
	1750	SX	Glasgow C.–Birmingham N.S.

86.227:	0556	SX	Wolverhampton–Euston	
	0740	SO	Northampton–Euston	
	1000		Euston–Carlisle	
	1454		Carlisle–Euston	1055 from Stranraer Hbr.
	2210	SX	Euston–Wolverhampton	
86.228:	0810	SX	Glasgow C.÷Euston	
	1814	SX	Euston–Northampton	
86.229:	0740	SX	Manchester P.–Mitre Bridge Jn.	
	1118	SX	Willesden WL Jn.–Manchester P.	0952 from Brighton.
	1740	SX	Manchester P.–Euston	
	2340	SX	Euston–Wolverhampton	
86.230:	1155	SO	Manchester P.–Mitre Bridge Jn.	
	1958	SO	Willesden WL Jn.–Manchester P.	1825 from Brighton.
86.231:	0630	SX	Wolverhampton–Euston	
	0945	SX	Euston–Liverpool L.S.	
	1752	FO	Liverpool L.S.–Euston	
	1815	FSX	Liverpool L.S.–Euston	
	2200	SX	Euston–Crewe	
86.232:	0656	SO	Wolverhampton–Euston	
	1200	SO	Euston–Preston	
	1709	SO	Preston–Euston	1630 from Blackpool N.
86.233:	1656	SO	Wolverhampton–Euston	
	2010	SO	Euston–Northampton	
86.234:	1517	SO	Birmingham Int.–Manchester P.	
86.235:	0900*	SO	Euston–Preston	
	1417	SO	Preston–Euston	1338 from Blackpool N.
	1950	SO	Euston–Liverpool L.S.	
86.236:	0825	SO	Liverpool L.S.–Euston	
	1609	SO	Willesden WL Jn.–Liverpool L.S.	1355 from Dover W.D.
86.237:	0750	SO	Euston–Liverpool L.S.	
	1315	SO	Liverpool L.S.–Euston	
	1740	SO	Euston–Wolverhampton	
86.238:	1550	SO	Glasgow C.–Preston	
86.239:	0902	SO	Northampton–Euston	
86.240:	0354	SO	Crewe–Mitre Bridge Jn.	0305 from Manchester P.
	0803	SO	Willesden WL Jn.–Manchester P.	0635 from Brighton.
	1335	SO	Manchester P.–Euston	
	1735	SO	Euston–Crewe	
	2105	SO	Crewe–Euston	
86.241:	1326	SO	Manchester P.–Birmingham N.S.	
	1551	SO	Birmingham N.S.–Liverpool L.S.	
86.242:	0238	SO	Carlisle–Euston	2240 from Stranraer Hbr.
	0940	SO	Euston–Wolverhampton	
	1256	SO	Wolverhampton–Euston	
	2050	SO	Euston–Liverpool L.S.	
86.243:	1426	SO	Wolverhampton–Euston	
86.244:	1226	SO	Wolverhampton–Euston	1133 from Shrewsbury.
	1710	SO	Euston–Liverpool L.S.	
86.245:	0920	SO	Liverpool L.S.–Birmingham N.S.	
	1139	SO	Birmingham N.S.–Liverpool L.S.	
	1900	SO	Liverpool L.S.–Birmingham N.S.	
86.246:	0735	SO	Manchester P.–Euston	
	1130	SO	Euston–Crewe	
	1514	SO	Crewe–Euston	1255 from Holyhead.
	1850	SO	Euston–Crewe	
86.247:	0556	SO	Wolverhampton–Euston	
	0925	SO	Euston–Northampton	
	1102	SO	Northampton–Euston	
	1320	SO	Euston–Manchester P.	
	1855	SO	Manchester P.–Euston	

86.248:	0700	SO	Glasgow C.–Ayr	
	0845	SO	Ayr–Glasgow C.	
	1050	SO	Glasgow C.–Birmingham N.S.	
	1710	SO	Birmingham N.S.–Glasgow C.	1027 from Penzance.
86.249:	1936	SUN	Crewe–Euston	1656 from Holyhead.
86.250:	1040	SUN	Euston–Wolverhampton	
	1430	SUN	Wolverhampton–Euston	
	1840	SUN	Euston–Wolverhampton	
86.251:	1535	SUN	Liverpool L.S.–Euston	
	2050	SUN	Euston–Liverpool L.S.	
86.252:	1525	SUN	Carlisle–Euston	
	2150	SUN	Euston–Manchester P.	
86.253:	1715*	SUN	Preston–Euston	
86.254:	1920	SUN	Liverpool L.S.–Birmingham N.S.	
	2155	SUN	Birmingham N.S.–Manchester P.	1732 from Poole.
86.255:	0850	SUN	Euston–Crewe	
	1557	SUN	Crewe–Euston	1305 from Holyhead.
	2020	SUN	Euston–Manchester P.	
86.256:	1330	SUN	Euston–Manchester P.	
	1915	SUN	Manchester P.–Euston	
	2350	SUN	Euston–Crewe	
86.257:	1523*	SUN	Preston–Glasgow C.	1406 from Manchester V.
	1945+	SUN	Glasgow C.–Preston	+ From 1/11
86.258:	1930	SUN	Liverpool L.S.–Euston	T.87.045
86.259:	1755	SUN	Manchester P.–Euston	
86.260:	1130	SUN	Euston–Stafford	
	1600	SUN	Stafford–Euston	1418 from Manchester P.
	1930	SUN	Euston–Preston	
86.261:	1603	SUN	Mitre Bridge Jn.–Liverpool L.S.	1345 from Dover W.D.
86.262:	1023*	SUN	Preston–Euston	P.47.526
	1100*	SUN	Preston–Euston	P.47.526
	1710	SUN	Euston–Wolverhampton	
	2026	SUN	Wolverhampton–Euston	
86.263:	0700	SUN	Wolverhampton–Mitre Bridge Jn.	
	1220	SUN	Willesden WL Jn.–Manchester P.	1053 from Brighton.
	1855	SUN	Manchester P.–Birmingham N.S.	
	2220	SUN	Birmingham N.S.–Liverpool L.S.	
86.264:	1858	SUN	Willesden WL Jn.–Manchester P.	1723 from Brighton.
86.265:	0800	SUN	Wolverhampton–Euston	
	1240	SUN	Euston–Wolverhampton	
	1656	SUN	Wolverhampton–Euston	
	2110	SUN	Euston–Wolverhampton	
86.266:	0030	SUN	Manchester P.–Euston	P.47.470
	1450	SUN	Euston–Liverpool L.S.	
86.267:	1820	SUN	Euston–Manchester P.	
86.268:	1006	SUN	Stafford–Euston	0820 from Manchester P.
	1500	SUN	Euston–Wolverhampton	
	1826	SUN	Wolverhampton–Euston	1733 from Shrewsbury.
	2340	SUN	Euston–Wolverhampton	
86.269:	0900	SUN	Wolverhampton–Euston	
	1400	SUN	Euston–Manchester P.	
	2140	SUN	Manchester P.–Birmingham N.S.	
86.270:	0153+	SUN	Crewe–Stafford	+ To 27/12
	1038	SUN	Stafford–Euston	0850 from Manchester P.
	1620	SUN	Euston–Liverpool L.S.	
86.271:	2103	SUN	Birmingham N.S.–Manchester P.	1810 from Paddington.
86.272:	0918	SUN	Crewe–Euston	T.87.050
86.273:	1701	SUN	Carstairs–Birmingham N.S.	1614 from Edinburgh.

86.274:	1700	SUN	Liverpool L.S.–Euston	T.86.450
	2140	SUN	Euston–Wolverhampton	
86.275:	0940	SUN	Euston–Wolverhampton	
	1335	SUN	Wolverhampton–Euston	
	1810	SUN	Euston–Wolverhampton	
86.401:	0820	SX	Liverpool L.S.–Euston	
	1220	SX	Euston–Liverpool L.S.	
86.402:	0042	MO	Manchester P.–Crewe	
86.403:	0132	SX	Mossend Yard–Euston	2130 from Inverness.
	1250	SX	Euston–Manchester P.	
	1806	SX	Manchester P.–Birmingham Int.	
	2037	SX	Birmingham Int.–Liverpool L.S.	
86.404:	0354	SX	Crewe–Mitre Bridge Jn.	0305 from Manchester P.
	0803	SX	Willesden WL Jn.–Manchester P.	0635 from Brighton.
	1300	SX	Manchester P.–Euston	
	1710	SX	Euston–Wolverhampton	
86.405:	1953	FO	Crewe–Liverpool L.S.	1735 from Euston.
86.406:	0238	SX	Carlisle–Euston	2240 from Stranraer Hbr.
	1300	SX	Euston–Glasgow C.	
86.407:	0150	SO	Mossend Yard–Euston	2130 from Inverness.
	0930	SO	Euston–Crewe	
	1855		Crewe–Euston	1623 from Holyhead.
	2350	SO	Euston–Crewe	
86.408:	0620		Manchester P.–Euston	
	1010	SX	Euston–Birmingham N.S.	
	1218	SX	Birmingham N.S.–Euston	
	1420	SO	Euston–Liverpool L.S.	
	1530	SX	Euston–Glasgow C.	
86.409:	0755	SX	Euston–Liverpool L.S.	
	1315	SX	Liverpool L.S.–Euston	
	1735	FSX	Euston–Crewe	
	1735	FO	Euston–Liverpool L.S.	
86.410:	1900	FO	Euston–Manchester P.	
86.411:	0250	MX	Crewe–Liverpool L.S.	2350 from Euston.
	0252	MO	Crewe–Liverpool L.S.	2350 from Euston.
	0705	SX	Liverpool L.S.–Euston	
	1320	FO	Euston–Liverpool L.S.	
	1350	FSX	Euston–Liverpool L.S.	
86.412:	1020		Euston–Manchester P.	
	1455	FSO	Manchester P.–Euston	
	1640	FX	Manchester P.–Mitre Bridge Jn.	
	1843	FO	Euston–Wolverhampton	
	2019	FX	Willesden WL Jn.–Manchester P.	1825 from Brighton.
	2355	FO	Birmingham N.S.–Glasgow C.	1838 from Paignton.
86.413:	2105	FSX	Crewe–Wolverhampton	
	2355	FSX	Birmingham N.S.–Glasgow C.	1838 from Paignton.
86.414:	1609	SX	Willesden WL Jn.–Liverpool L.S.	1355 from Dover W.D.
	2020	FO	Liverpool L.S.–Euston	
86.415:	1618	SX	Birmingham Int.–Euston	
	1900	FSX	Euston–Manchester P.	
	1953	FO	Willesden WL Jn.–Manchester P.	1754 from Dover W.D.
86.416:	1640	FO	Manchester P.–Mitre Bridge Jn.	
	2019	FO	Willesden WL Jn.–Manchester P.	1825 from Brighton.
86.417:	0725		Birmingham N.S.–Glasgow C.	
	1550	SX	Glasgow C.–Preston	
86.418:	1150	SX	Liverpool L.S.–Euston	
	1820	FO	Euston–Manchester P.	
	1953	FSX	Willesden WL Jn.–Manchester P.	1754 from Dover W.D.

86.419:	1430	FO	Euston–Liverpool L.S.
	1815	FO	Liverpool L.S.–Euston
86.420:	1550	SX	Euston–Liverpool L.S.
86.421:	0805	MO	Manchester P.–Euston	T.86.201
86.422:	0743	SO	Liverpool L.S.–Euston
	1250	SO	Euston–Liverpool L.S.
	2037	SO	Birmingham Int.–Liverpool L.S.
86.423:	1130	SO	Liverpool L.S.–Birmingham Int.
	1952	SO	Birmingham N.S.–Manchester P.
86.424:	1800	SO	Euston–Manchester P.
86.425:	1029	SO	Preston–Euston	0950 from Blackpool N.
	1540	SO	Euston–Wolverhampton
86.426:	1110	SO	Euston–Northampton
	1302	SO	Northampton–Euston
	1650	SO	Euston–Northampton
	1830	SO	Northampton–Euston
	2045	SO	Euston–Wolverhampton
86.427:	0723	SO	Manchester P.–Euston
	1810	SO	Euston–Northampton
86.428:	0950	SO	Liverpool L.S.–Euston
	1440	SO	Euston–Wolverhampton
	1826	SO	Wolverhampton–Euston
86.429:	1341*	SUN	Preston–Euston	P.47.474
	1423*	SUN	Preston–Euston
86.430:	1212	SUN	Stafford–Euston	1030 from Manchester P.
	1800	SUN	Euston–Liverpool L.S.
86.431:	1855	SUN	Birmingham N.S.–Glasgow C.	1425 from Plymouth.
86.432:	1936	SUN	Crewe–Euston	1656 from Holyhead.
86.433:	1313	SUN	Stafford–Euston	1130 from Manchester P.
	1910	SUN	Euston–Wolverhampton
86.434:	1610	SUN	Liverpool L.S.–Euston
86.435:	1121*	SUN	Crewe–Euston	0938 from Liverpool L.S.
	1121*	SUN	Crewe–Euston	0958 from Liverpool L.S.
	1650	SUN	Euston–Manchester P.
86.436:	1640+	SUN	Crewe–Euston	+ From 3/1
86.437:	1955	SUN	Birmingham N.S.–Liverpool L.S.	1548 from Southampton C.
86.438:	1526	SUN	Wolverhampton–Euston	1426 from Shrewsbury.
	1920	SUN	Euston–Manchester P.
86.439:	1430	SUN	Euston–Preston
	2023	SUN	Preston–Euston	1947 from Blackpool N.
86.440:	1216*	SUN	Crewe–Birmingham N.S.	1037 from Liverpool L.S.
	1216*	SUN	Crewe–Birmingham N.S.	1042 from Liverpool L.S.
	1423	SUN	Birmingham N.S.–Euston
	1850	SUN	Euston–Liverpool L.S.
86.441:	1010*	SUN	Crewe–Euston	0835 from Liverpool L.S.
	1010*	SUN	Crewe–Euston	0845 from Liverpool L.S.
	1520	SUN	Euston–Manchester P.
86.442:	1620	SUN	Birmingham N.S.–Glasgow C.	1148 from Southampton C.
86.443:	1610	SUN	Euston–Manchester P.
86.444:	0123	SUN	Carlisle–Euston	P.47.582
	1050	SUN	Euston–Crewe
	1605*	SUN	Crewe–Euston	1429 from Liverpool L.S.
	1605*	SUN	Crewe–Euston	1439 from Liverpool L.S.
	1950	SUN	Euston–Liverpool L.S.

86.445:	0324	SUN	Carlisle–Euston	P.47.472
	1200+	SUN	Euston–Crewe	+ to 27/12
	1200+	SUN	Euston–Preston	+ From 3/1 P.47.526
	1640+	SUN	Crewe–Euston	+ to 27/12
	1715+	SUN	Preston–Euston	+ From 3/1
86.446:	1800	SUN	Manchester P.–Euston	
86.447:	1830	SUN	Euston–Carlisle	
86.448:	1000*	SUN	Euston–Preston	P.47.474
	1550*	SUN	Preston–Euston	
86.449:	0302	SUN	Crewe–Euston	M.87.057
86.450:	1700	SUN	Liverpool L.S.–Euston	T.86.275

CLASS 87

The booked power for the majority of Anglo-Scottish trains via the West Coast route, also for the more important other services on this line.

87.001:	0030		Mossend Yard–Euston	1740 from Fort William.
	0910	SX	Euston–Birmingham N.S.	
	1118	SX	Birmingham N.S.–Euston	
	1400	SX	Euston–Glasgow C.	
	1825	SO	Euston–Carlisle	
	2350	SX	Glasgow C.–Birmingham N.S.	
87.002:	0756		Wolverhampton–Euston	
	1120		Euston–Liverpool L.S.	
	1605		Liverpool L.S.–Euston	
	2055	SX	Euston–Mossend Yard	
	2240	SO	Euston–Carlisle	
87.003:	0700	SX	Glasgow C.–Ayr	
	0845	SX	Ayr–Glasgow C.	
	1050	SX	Glasgow C.–Birmingham N.S.	
	1710	SX	Birmingham N.S.–Glasgow C.	1027 from Penzance.
87.004:	0054	SX	Carstairs–Euston	2355 from Edinburgh.
	0940	SX	Euston–Wolverhampton	
	1040	SO	Euston–Wolverhampton	
	1326	SO	Wolverhampton–Euston	
	1426	SX	Wolverhampton–Euston	
	1740	SX	Euston–Manchester P.	
	1820	SO	Euston–Liverpool L.S.	
87.005:	0600		Glasgow C.–Euston	
	1340	SX	Euston–Wolverhampton	
	1400	SO	Euston–Glasgow C.	
	1656	SX	Wolverhampton–Euston	
	2010	SX	Euston–Wolverhampton	
87.006:	1010		Glasgow C.–Euston	0845 from Ayr.
	1650	SX	Euston–Liverpool L.S.	
	1700	SO	Euston–Manchester P.	
87.007:	1030	SO	Manchester P.–Euston	
	1617	SO	Euston–Crewe	
	1954	SO	Crewe–Birmingham N.S.	1710 from Holyhead.
87.008:	0900	SX	Euston–Preston	
	1458	SX	Preston–Euston	1422 from Blackpool N.
	1910	SX	Euston–Wolverhampton	
87.009:	0755	SO	Coventry–Crewe	
	0810	SX	Euston–Birmingham N.S.	
	1018	SX	Birmingham N.S.–Euston	
	1138	SO	Crewe–Euston	0856 from Holyhead.
	1520		Euston–Manchester P.	
	2000	SX	Manchester P.–Euston	
	2345	SX	Euston–Carstairs	

87.010:	0850		Glasgow C.–Birmingham N.S.
	1458		Birmingham N.S.–Glasgow C.	1028 from Plymouth.
	2310	SX	Glasgow C.–Euston
87.011:	1430	SX	Manchester P.–Euston
	1830	SX	Euston–Carlisle
87.012:	0124		Carlisle–Euston	2215 from Glasgow C.
	0820		Euston–Manchester P.
	1326	SX	Manchester P.–Birmingham N.S.
	1551	SX	Birmingham N.S.–Liverpool L.S.
	1640	SO	Manchester P.–Mitre Bridge Jn.
	1920	SX	Liverpool L.S.–Euston
	2019	SO	Willesden WL Jn.–Manchester P.	1825 from Brighton.
	2300	SX	Euston–Carlisle
87.013:	0600		Carlisle–Euston
	1150	SO	Euston–Manchester P.
	1420	SX	Euston–Manchester P.
	1855	SX	Manchester P.–Euston
	1806	SO	Manchester P.–Birmingham Int.
	2037	SO	Birmingham Int.–Liverpool L.S.
87.014:	0656	SX	Wolverhampton–Euston
87.015:	0735	SX	Manchester P.–Euston
	1610	SX	Euston–Birmingham N.S.
	1818	SX	Birmingham N.S.–Euston
	2330	SX	Euston–Glasgow C.
87.016:	0840	SO	Euston–Carstairs
	0855	SX	Euston–Carstairs
	1710		Glasgow C.–Euston
87.017:	0833		Crewe–Euston	0605 from Holyhead.
	1210	SX	Euston–Birmingham N.S.
	1240	SO	Euston–Wolverhampton
	1418	SX	Birmingham N.S.–Euston
	1526	SO	Wolverhampton–Euston
	1850	SX	Euston–Crewe
	1930	SO	Euston–Preston
87.018:	1210	SX	Glasgow C.–Euston
	2230	SX	Euston–Mossend Yard
87.019:	0332		Crewe–Euston	0115 from Holyhead.
	0730		Euston–Glasgow C.
	1524		Carstairs–Euston	1030 from Inverness.
	2350	FO	Euston–Crewe
87.020:	0755	SX	Coventry–Crewe
	0810	SO	Glasgow C.–Euston
	1138	SX	Crewe–Euston	0856 from Holyhead.
	1730		Euston–Glasgow C.
87.021:	0750	SX	Euston–Manchester P.
	1155	SX	Manchester P.–Mitre Bridge Jn.
87.022:	0930		Manchester P.–Euston
	1500	SO	Euston–Manchester P.
	1510	SX	Euston–Wolverhampton
	1826	SX	Wolverhampton–Euston
	1920	SO	Manchester P.–Birmingham N.S.
	2210	SO	Birmingham N.S.–Liverpool L.S.	1732 from Poole.
87.023:	1029	SX	Preston–Euston	0950 from Blackpool N.
	1700	SX	Euston–Manchester P.
87.024:	1030	SX	Manchester P.–Euston
	1600	SX	Euston–Manchester P.
87.025:	0726	SX	Wolverhampton–Euston
	1030		Euston–Glasgow C.
	1750	SO	Glasgow C.–Birmingham N.S.

87.026:	0054	SO	Carstairs–Euston	2355 from Edinburgh.
	0945	SO	Euston–Liverpool L.S.	
	1500	SO	Liverpool L.S.–Euston	
	1920	SO	Euston–Manchester P.	
87.027:	0720	SO	Glasgow C.–Birmingham N.S.	
	1259	SO	Birmingham N.S.–Glasgow C.	0834 from Poole.
87.028:	0926	SO	Wolverhampton–Euston	
	1300	SO	Euston–Glasgow C.	
87.029:	1210	SO	Glasgow C.–Euston	
	1940	SO	Euston–Wolverhampton	
	2355	SO	Birmingham N.S.–Carlisle	P.47.582
87.030:	0740	SO	Manchester P.–Mitre Bridge Jn.	
	1118	SO	Willesden WL Jn.–Manchester P.	0952 from Brighton.
	1800	SO	Manchester P.–Euston	
	2150	SO	Euston–Crewe	
87.031:	0825	SO	Preston–Glasgow C.	0735 from Manchester V.
	1410	SO	Glasgow C.–Euston	
	2200	SO	Euston–Carlisle	
87.032:	0659	SO	Preston–Euston	0620 from Blackpool N.
	1530	SO	Euston–Glasgow C.	
87.033:	1630	SO	Manchester P.–Euston	
	2055	SO	Euston–Carlisle	
87.034:	1300	SUN	Euston–Glasgow C.	
87.035:	1000	SUN	Wolverhampton–Euston	
	1730	SUN	Euston–Glasgow C.	
87.036:	1601	SUN	Preston–Euston	1519 from Blackpool N.
	2105	SUN	Euston–Carlisle	
87.037:	0302*	SUN	Crewe–Euston	M.86.449
	0349*	SUN	Crewe–Euston	M.86.449
	0930	SUN	Euston–Stafford	
	1453	SUN	Stafford–Euston	1305 from Manchester P.
	1940	SUN	Euston–Wolverhampton	
87.038:	1539	SUN	Manchester P.–Mitre Bridge Jn.	
	2230	SUN	Euston–Mossend Yard	
87.039:	1710	SUN	Glasgow C.–Euston	
	2345	SUN	Euston–Carstairs	
87.040:	1323*	SUN	Crewe–Euston	1146 from Liverpool L.S.
	1323*	SUN	Crewe–Euston	1159 from Liverpool L.S.
	1900	SUN	Euston–Crewe	
87.041:	1632	SUN	Carlisle–Euston	1410 from Glasgow C.
	2240	SUN	Euston–Wolverhampton	
87.042:	1610	SUN	Glasgow C.–Euston	
	2300	SUN	Euston–Carlisle	
87.043:	1230*	SUN	Birmingham N.S.–Glasgow C.	P.47.582
	1322*	SUN	Birmingham N.S.–Glasgow C.	
	2310	SUN	Glasgow C.–Euston	
87.044:	0143	SUN	Carlisle–Birmingham N.S.	P.47.474
	1218	SUN	Birmingham N.S.–Euston	0935 from Manchester P.
	1700	SUN	Euston–Crewe	
87.045:	0112	SUN	Carlisle–Euston	P.47.526
	1250	SUN	Euston–Liverpool L.S.	
	1930	SUN	Liverpool L.S.–Euston	T.86.258
87.046:	1815	SUN	Liverpool L.S.–Euston	
	2200	SUN	Euston–Crewe	
87.047:	1555	SUN	Manchester P.–Euston	
	2010	SUN	Euston–Wolverhampton	

87.048:	2350	SUN	Glasgow C.–Birmingham N.S.	
87.049:	1650	SUN	Manchester P.–Euston	
	2055	SUN	Euston–Mossend Yard	
87.050:	0918*	SUN	Crewe–Euston	T.86.272
	0918*	SUN	Crewe–Euston	T.86.272
	1530	SUN	Euston–Glasgow C.	
87.051:	0810	SUN	Euston–Crewe	
	1532*	SUN	Crewe–Euston	1321 from Llandudno Junction.
	1532*	SUN	Crewe–Euston	1300 from Llandudno Junction.
	2330	SUN	Euston–Glasgow C.	
87.052:	1715	SUN	Liverpool L.S.–Birmingham N.S.	
	1925	SUN	Birmingham N.S.–Manchester P.	
87.053:	1720	SUN	Glasgow C.–Birmingham N.S.	
	2355	SUN	Birmingham N.S.–Glasgow C.	2125 from Bristol T.M.
87.054:	1140	SUN	Euston–Wolverhampton	
	1556	SUN	Wolverhampton–Euston	
	2210	SUN	Euston–Manchester P.	
87.055:	1630	SUN	Euston–Lancaster	
	2338	SUN	Preston–Stafford	2149 from Barrow in Furness.

CLASS 89

Although the only member of this class has now been in service for several months, it has yet to make an appearance on a scheduled passenger service. The only occasion that fare paying passengers have been hauled (contrary to stories in the railway press) has been in an emergency when a test train was used to convey otherwise stranded passengers. However, it is expected to make its passenger service debut in the not too distant future.

CLASS 90

The first member of this class has now appeared from the manufacturers and should enter service on the West Coast Main line during the currency of this timetable.

CLASS 91

The first member of this class should appear early in 1988 and passenger service on the East Coast Main line is expected during the currency of this timetable.

CLASS 97

This class consists of various types of locomotive allocated to departmental use. These locomotives do not normally haul revenue earning trains over BR metals and their only use on passenger services would be to clear the running line in the event of a failure.

CLASS 98

This heading is taken to mean the BR owned Vale of Rheidol narrow gauge locomotives rather than the privately owned steam locomotives allocated TOPS numbers. During the winter timetable period there are no scheduled services over this line and the locomotives are only used if required for specials.

INDEX OF LOCOMOTIVE HAULED TRAINS

Aberdeen

1A77	0435		Inverness	47.514
1T06	0525	SX	Glasgow Q.S.	47.707
1T08	0525	SO	Glasgow Q.S.	47.707
2A72	0625	SX	Inverurie	47.513
1T10	0700		Glasgow Q.S.	47.708
1C67	0730	SX	Carstairs	47.588
1H25	0740		Inverness	47.503
1H27	0940		Inverness	47.657
1V94	1030	SUN	Penzance	47.459 47.601
				50.055
1B38	1040		Edinburgh	47.654
1T78	1100	SUN	Glasgow Q.S.	47.712
1T22	1105		Glasgow Q.S.	47.705
1H29	1140		Inverness	47.514
1B32	1240		Edinburgh	47.707
1T82	1300	SUN	Glasgow Q.S.	47.714
1T26	1305		Glasgow Q.S.	47.706
1H55	1310	SUN	Inverness	47.520
1H31	1340		Inverness	47.502
1B40	1405	SO	Edinburgh	47.653
1B40	1445	SX	Edinburgh	47.653
1T84	1500	SUN	Glasgow Q.S.	47.711

1T32	1505		Glasgow Q.S	47.708
1B74	1530	SUN	Edinburgh	47.715
1H33	1540		Inverness	47.590 47.503
1H57	1540	SUN	Inverness	47.524
2A73	1625	SX	Dyce	47.657
1T86	1700	SUN	Glasgow Q.S.	47.713
1T38	1705		Glasgow Q.S.	47.709
1A75	1710		Huntly	47.650
1H35	1755		Inverness	47.512 47.504
1B78	1835	SUN	Edinburgh	47.419
1T90	1900	SUN	Glasgow Q.S.	47.716
1E43	2000	SX	King's Cross	47.657
1E43	2000	SUN	King's Cross	47.663
1H59	2010	SUN	Inverness	47.522
1E43	2025	SO	King's Cross	47.657
1B42	2030		Edinburgh	47.707
1H37	2055		Inverness	47.502
1E48	2115	SX	King's Cross	47.650
1E48	2115	SUN	King's Cross	47.661
1L32	2235	SX	Perth	47.706
1L32	2235	SUN	Perth	47.714

Aberystwyth

1A31	0714		Euston	37.401 47.545
				86.220 86.224

Arbroath

2Y02	1924		Dundee	47.515

Ayr

1M20	0845		Euston	87.006 87.003
				86.248

Banbury

1V21	0707	SX	Paddington	50.007

Barrow in Furness

1K12	2149	SUN	Stafford	47.475 47.526
				87.055

1K12	2149	SX	Stafford	47.441 85.001

Basingstoke

2V06	0635	SX	Sherborne	33.106 33.107
2V26	0734	SUN	Reading G.	33.110
1V08	0826	SUN	Exeter St. D.	50.044

1V08	0826	SUN	Honiton	50.044
2L11	0839	SO	Salisbury	33.107

Birmingham Int.

1H88	1517		Manchester P.	86.204 86.234
1A20	1618	SX	Euston	86.415

1F48	2037		Liverpool L.S.	86.403 86.422
				87.013

Birmingham N.S.

1A15	0638	SX	Euston	87.017
1S53	0725		Glasgow C.	86.417
1A82	0740	SX	Euston	86.211
1E66	0820	SX	Norwich	31.403
1E66	0821	SO	Norwich	31.426
1P06	0830	SUN	Preston	47.476
1D54	0900	SUN	Llandudno Jn.	47.462
1A28	1018	SX	Euston	87.009
1E72	1039		Norwich	31.421 31.404
1A34	1118	SX	Euston	87.001
1F12	1139		Liverpool L.S.	86.205 86.245
1A39	1218	SX	Euston	86.408
1E99	1220		Cambridge	31.425
1S61	1230	SUN	Glasgow C.	47.582 87.043
1V69	1310	SX	Paddington	50.013
1V51	1310	SO	Paddington	50.013
1A44	1318	SX	Euston	86.211
1S61	1322	SUN	Glasgow C.	87.043

1A48	1418	SX	Euston	87.017
1E76	1420		Ipswich	31.424
1A38	1423	SUN	Euston	86.440
1V75	1440	SX	Paddington	50.012
1V41	1440	SO	Paddington	50.012
1A54	1518	SX	Euston	86.210
1E54	1540		Cambridge	31.452
1F14	1551		Liverpool L.S.	87.012 86.241
1A60	1618	SX	Euston	86.223
1E80	1620		Norwich	31.423
1E77	1720	SUN	Norwich	31.427
1A71	1818	SX	Euston	87.015
1E31	1818	SUN	Harwich P.Q.	47.418 86.132
1E82	1830		Norwich	31.422
1E78	1830	SUN	Ipswich	31.429
1H47	1925	SUN	Manchester P.	87.052
1H28	1952	SO	Manchester P.	86.423
1E68	2035	FO	Cambridge	31.420

Blackpool N.

1A12 0620		Euston	47.438 86.218 87.032	1M51 1120		Nottingham	47.640
1E86 0720		Harwich P.Q.	31.402 47.444	1A62 1338	SO	Euston	47.438 86.235
1A15 0948	SUN	Euston	47.483 47.526 86.262	1A62 1422	SX	Euston	47.440 87.008
1A26 0950		Euston	47.441 87.023 86.425	1A53 1519	SUN	Euston	47.478 87.036
1A15 1019	SUN	Euston	47.483 86.262	1A75 1630		Euston	47.440 86.202 86.232
				1M54 1944		Nottingham	47.641
				1A54 1947	SUN	Euston	47.483 86.439

Bletchley

1A55 0749	SX	Euston	86.210

Bournemouth

2B12 0559	SUN	Waterloo	33.112	1B30 1558	SUN	Waterloo	73.122
2W01 0616		Weymouth	33.102	1B30 1600		Waterloo	73.111
2W03 0716		Weymouth	33.101	1B32 1700		Waterloo	73.109
2B20 0725	SX	Eastleigh	73.113	2W07 1746	SX	Weymouth	33.104
1B14 0900		Waterloo	73.112	1W40 1758	SUN	Waterloo	73.121
1B18 1000		Waterloo	73.111	1B36 1858	SUN	Waterloo	73.120
2W11 1018	SUN	Weymouth	33.116	1B36 1900	SX	Waterloo	73.114
1B20 1100		Waterloo	73.109	2B54 2140	SX	Waterloo	73.111
1B26 1400		Waterloo	73.110	2B58 2300	SO	Eastleigh	33.101
1B28 1500		Waterloo	73.112				

Brighton

1M34 0635		Manchester P.	47.534 86.404 86.240	1V12 1112	SO	Exeter St. D.	33.019
				1V12 1112	SO	Paignton	50.034
1V46 0830		Cardiff C.	33.010 47.557 47.414 47.556	1M00 1322		Liverpool L.S.	47.534 86.222
1M50 0952		Manchester P.	47.535 86.229 87.030	1V85 1612	SUN	Cardiff C.	33.026 33.036
				1V18 1712	SUN	Exeter St. D.	47.586
1V58 1012	SUN	Cardiff C.	33.028	1M15 1723	SUN	Manchester P.	47.566 86.264
1V58 1012	SUN	Westbury	33.034	1M13 1825		Manchester P.	47.534 86.416 86.412 86.230 87.012
1Y58 1012	SUN	Salisbury	33.037				
1M50 1053	SUN	Manchester P.	47.567 86.263				

Bristol T.M.

1B86 0124		Swansea	47.550	2C44 1648		Weston Super Mare	47.414 47.553 50.027
2A01 0500		Yeovil P.M.	33.006	2C46 1713		Taunton	50.023
1C09 0635		Plymouth	50.026 50.022	1A79 1930	SUN	Paddington	50.050
2B72 0720		Swansea	47.552	2O98 2015		Portsmouth Hbr.	33.012 33.019
1O35 1006	SUN	Portsmouth Hbr.	33.023	1S19 2125	SUN	Glasgow C.	37.003 47.571 87.053
1O35 1008		Portsmouth Hbr.	47.555 33.006				
1O40 1208	SUN	Portsmouth Hbr.	33.037	1O50 2145	SX	Southampton C.	33.010
1O42 1405	SUN	Portsmouth Hbr.	33.034	2B80 2207	SO	Cardiff C.	33.006
1B31 1450	SUN	Cardiff C.	33.033	1C80 2235	SX	Exeter St. D.	50.023
1O43 1600	SUN	Portsmouth Hbr.	33.027	1A86 2310	FO	Swindon	50.009
2B36 1600	SUN	Cardiff C.	33.036				
2O60 1615		Weymouth	33.005				

Burton-on-Trent

1E82 0649		Sheffield	31.451

Cambridge

1M60 0525		Birmingham N.S.	31.452	1H19 1105		Liverpool St.	86.107
1M66 0603	SX	Birmingham N.S.	31.421	1H19 1215	SUN	Liverpool St.	86.120
1H11 0655	SO	Liverpool St.	86.107	1H23 1305		Liverpool St.	86.102
1H11 0705	SX	Liverpool St.	86.107	1H27 1505		Liverpool St.	86.107
2H02 0720	SX	King's Lynn	47.421	1M76 1613		Birmingham N.S.	31.420
2H02 0726	SO	King's Lynn	47.421	1H31 1705		Liverpool St.	86.102
1H13 0803	SX	Liverpool St.	86.103	2H18 1913		Peterborough	31.452
2H06 1018	SUN	King's Lynn	47.423				

Canterbury E.

1M02 0904		Liverpool L.S.	47.542 86.217

Cardiff C.

1O31 0550		Portsmouth Hbr.	33.012 47.555 33.005 33.008	1O33 0800		Portsmouth Hbr.	47.551 33.013 33.007
1M68 0607		Crewe	47.559	1A20 0815	SUN	Westbury	33.030 33.034
1O32 0630		Portsmouth Hbr.	47.556 33.009 33.005	1O36 1010		Portsmouth Hbr.	33.004 33.014 33.020 47.556

Train	Time	Days	Destination	Loco(s)		Train	Time	Days	Destination	Loco(s)	
1A31	1015	SUN	Westbury	33.027	33.028	1M75	1535		Crewe	47.558	
1M84	1045		Crewe	37.404		1O45	1600	SUN	Portsmouth Hbr.	33.030	37.405
1O40	1110	SUN	Portsmouth Hbr.	33.033		1O45	1620		Portsmouth Hbr.	33.006	33.012
1O41	1206	SO	Portsmouth Hbr.	33.002	33.014					33.011	33.002
1O41	1208	SX	Portsmouth Hbr.	33.006	33.010					47.585	
1M86	1300		Holyhead	47.435		1M86	1635	SUN	Holyhead	33.028	33.033
1O42	1305		Portsmouth Hbr.	33.001	33.011	1O96	1655	SUN	Brighton	47.559	
1M84	1350	SUN	Manchester P.	47.583		1M01	1735		Holyhead	33.023	33.036
1O43	1400		Portsmouth Hbr.	47.557	33.011	1O47	1806	SUN	Portsmouth Hbr.	33.007	33.003
				47.414	33.010	1O47	1810		Portsmouth Hbr.	33.020	
				47.556		1M73	1835		Crewe	47.403	
1O42	1400	SUN	Portsmouth Hbr.	33.034	33.036	1O48	1902	SUN	Portsmouth Hbr.	33.024	33.037
1O43	1453	SUN	Portsmouth Hbr.	33.024		1M82	2002		Crewe	47.550	47.552
1O85	1510		Brighton	33.006	33.009	1O49	2100	SUN	Portsmouth & S.	33.031	37.405
				33.008	47.564	1C82	2305	SUN	Bristol T.M.	33.036	

Carlisle

Train	Time	Days	Destination	Loco(s)		Train	Time	Days	Destination	Loco(s)
1S90	0555		Glasgow C.	47.593		1S37	1352		Glasgow C.	47.592
1A18	0600		Euston	87.013		1S37	1352	SUN	Glasgow C.	47.527
1E01	0630		Leeds	47.507		1A37	1525	SUN	Euston	86.252
1S50	0748		Glasgow C.	47.594		1E33	1615		Leeds	47.507
1E20	1005		Leeds	47.642		1E46	1745		Leeds	47.642
1S65	1155		Glasgow C.	47.506		1S88	1755		Glasgow C.	47.594
1E28	1237		Leeds	47.508		1S88	1935	SUN	Glasgow C.	47.603

Carmarthen

Train	Time	Days	Destination	Loco(s)	
1C82	2044	SX	Bristol T.M.	47.552	47.554

Carstairs

Train	Time	Days	Destination	Loco(s)		Train	Time	Days	Destination	Loco(s)	
1B03	0459		Edinburgh	47.516	47.505	1B67	1808	SUN	Edinburgh	47.519	
1L41	0529		Perth	47.587		1B69	1832	SUN	Edinburgh	47.601	
1B09	1149	SX	Edinburgh	47.589		1A69	1859		Aberdeen	47.511	47.511
1B13	1346		Edinburgh	47.588	47.499	1A02	2033	SUN	Aberdeen	47.602	
1B21	1609		Edinburgh	47.589	47.511	1B29	2144		Edinburgh	47.499	
1B19	1717		Edinburgh	47.595	47.499	1B71	2306	SUN	Edinburgh	47.532	

Clapham Jn.

Train	Time	Days	Destination	Loco(s)	Train	Time	Days	Destination	Loco(s)
2M66	1600	SX	Kensington O.	33.106	2M68	1650	SX	Kensington O.	33.106
2M67	1625	SX	Kensington O.	33.106	2M69	1715	SX	Kensington O.	33.106

Cleethorpes

Train	Time	Days	Destination	Loco(s)	Train	Time	Days	Destination	Loco(s)
1M16	0610		Liverpool L.S.	31.401	1M19	1120	SUN	Liverpool L.S.	31.413

Colchester

Train	Time	Days	Destination	Loco(s)
1P12	1033	SUN	Norwich	47.426

Coventry

Train	Time	Days	Destination	Loco(s)		Train	Time	Days	Destination	Loco(s)
1D33	0755		Holyhead	47.432	87.020	1P02	0828	SO	Lancaster	86.208
				87.009						

Crewe

Train	Time	Days	Destination	Loco(s)	Train	Time	Days	Destination	Loco(s)
1V01	0204	MX	Cardiff C.	47.551	1V09	1719		Cardiff C.	37.404
1V02	0620		Cardiff C.	37.404	1G42	2105	FSX	Wolverhampton	86.413
1V06	1135		Cardiff C.	47.559	1A74	2105	SO	Euston	86.240
1V11	1340	SUN	Swansea	37.406	1V11	2109		Cardiff C.	47.558

Crianlarich

Train	Time	Days	Destination	Loco(s)
2Y91	2000	SUN	Oban	37.418

Derby

Train	Time	Days	Destination	Loco(s)
1C22	1215	SUN	St. Pancras	47.486

Didcot Parkway

Train	Time	Days	Destination	Loco(s)	Train	Time	Days	Destination	Loco(s)
1F01	0902	SUN	Paddington	50.049	1F23	0921	SX	Paddington	50.012

Dover W.D.

Train	Time	Days	Destination	Loco(s)		Train	Time	Days	Destination	Loco(s)	
1M04	1345	SUN	Liverpool L.S.	47.575	86.261	1M31	1750		Manchester P.	47.535	86.415
1M22	1355	SX	Liverpool L.S.	47.533	86.414					86.418	
1M04	1355	SO	Liverpool L.S.	47.533	86.236						

Dunbar

Train	Time	Days	Destination	Loco(s)
2Y25	1848	SX	Edinburgh	47.589

Dunblane

2P14	0708	SX	Edinburgh	47.701

Dundee

1C65	0700		Carstairs	47.589 47.518	1T74	0825	SUN	Glasgow Q.S.	47.713
1J48	0715	SX	Edinburgh	47.415					

Dyce

1T14	0845		Glasgow Q.S.	47.709	1T48	1845		Glasgow Q.S.	47.702
2A80	1727	SX	Montrose	47.657					

Eastleigh

1W05	0715	SUN	Weymouth	33.112	2W05	0758	SUN	Weymouth	33.111 33.112

Edinburgh

2K31	0615	SX	Kirkcaldy	47.706	1O43	1700		Glasgow Q.S.	47.701
1O03	0700		Glasgow Q.S.	47.703	2J29	1713		Dundee	47.710
1H05	0710		Inverness	47.512	1C92	1714	SUN	Carstairs	47.602
1C62	0714		Carstairs	47.499	1O45	1730		Glasgow Q.S.	47.705
1O05	0730		Glasgow Q.S.	47.702	1O87	1730	SUN	Glasgow Q.S.	47.719
2O71	0736	SX	Glasgow Q.S.	47.500	1C72	1744		Carstairs	47.511 47.518
1O07	0800		Glasgow Q.S.	47.704	2Y24	1755	SX	Dunbar	47.589
1O09	0830		Glasgow Q.S.	47.701	1O47	1800		Glasgow Q.S.	47.703
1A55	0830		Aberdeen	47.706	1O89	1800	SUN	Glasgow Q.S.	47.717
1O11	0900		Glasgow Q.S.	47.703	1O49	1830		Glasgow Q.S.	47.704
1O13	0930		Glasgow Q.S.	47.702	1O01	1830	SUN	Glasgow Q.S.	47.718
1O71	0930	SUN	Glasgow Q.S.	47.717	1C73	1844		Carstairs	47.499
1O07	0950	SUN	Poole	47.481	1O51	1900		Glasgow Q.S.	47.701
1O15	1000		Glasgow Q.S.	47.704	1O91	1900	SUN	Glasgow Q.S.	47.720
1A47	1030		Aberdeen	47.653	1O53	1930		Glasgow Q.S.	47.705
1O17	1030		Glasgow Q.S.	47.701	1O63	1930	SUN	Glasgow Q.S.	47.719
1A83	1030	SUN	Aberdeen	47.715	1C93	1939	SUN	Carstairs	47.519
1O73	1030	SUN	Glasgow Q.S.	47.720	1A69	1955	SX	Aberdeen	47.587
1O19	1100		Glasgow Q.S.	47.703	1O55	2000		Glasgow Q.S.	47.703
1H11	1125		Inverness	47.505	1O93	2000	SUN	Glasgow Q.S.	47.717
1O21	1130		Glasgow Q.S.	47.702	1E10	2010	SX	King's Cross	47.654 47.655
1O75	1130	SUN	Glasgow Q.S.	47.719	1E10	2010	SUN	King's Cross	47.664 47.665
1C68	1140		Carstairs	47.511	1O57	2030		Glasgow Q.S.	47.704
1O23	1200		Glasgow Q.S.	47.704	1O69	2030	SUN	Glasgow Q.S.	47.718
1O25	1230		Glasgow Q.S.	47.701	1O59	2100		Glasgow Q.S.	47.701
1O77	1230	SUN	Glasgow Q.S.	47.717	1O95	2100	SUN	Glasgow Q.S.	47.720
1O27	1300		Glasgow Q.S.	47.703	1A99	2125	SUN	Aberdeen	47.601
1O29	1330		Glasgow Q.S.	47.710	1O61	2130		Glasgow Q.S.	47.705
1O79	1330	SUN	Glasgow Q.S.	47.720	1O97	2130	SUN	Glasgow Q.S.	47.719
1O31	1400		Glasgow Q.S.	47.702	1O63	2200	SO	Glasgow Q.S.	47.703
1A49	1427		Aberdeen	47.650	1O65	2230		Glasgow Q.S.	47.703 47.704
1O33	1430		Glasgow Q.S.	47.704	1M23	2235	SO	Euston	47.526 87.045
1A89	1430	SUN	Aberdeen	47.419	1O67	2300		Glasgow Q.S.	47.701
1O81	1430	SUN	Glasgow Q.S.	47.719	1O99	2300	SUN	Glasgow Q.S.	47.720
1O35	1500		Glasgow Q.S.	47.701	1C79	2304	SO	Carstairs	47.501
1O37	1530		Glasgow Q.S.	47.705	1H01	2325	SX	Inverness	47.514
1O83	1530	SUN	Glasgow Q.S.	47.717	1L75	2325	SO	Perth	47.514
1C84	1544		Carstairs	47.595 47.499	1H01	2325	SUN	Inverness	47.530
1O39	1600		Glasgow Q.S.	47.703	1C77	2344	SX	Carstairs	47.589
1M49	1614	SUN	Birmingham N.S.	47.519 47.601 86.273	1C79	2344	SO	Carstairs	47.501
					1C77	2344	SUN	Carstairs	47.602
1O41	1630		Glasgow Q.S.	47.704	1M23	2355	SX	Euston	87.004 87.026
1O85	1630	SUN	Glasgow Q.S.	47.720	1M23	2355	SUN	Euston	47.529 87.004
1A65	1655		Aberdeen	47.707					

Euston

1H04	0650		Manchester P.	86.216	1S59	0840	SO	Inverness	47.518 47.595 87.016
1P02	0710	SX	Lancaster	86.208					
1S47	0730		Glasgow C.	87.019	1D58	0850	SUN	Holyhead	47.465 86.255
1J20	0740		Shrewsbury	47.453 86.213 47.429 86.206	1S59	0855	SX	Inverness	47.511 47.588 87.016
1H05	0750	SX	Manchester P.	87.021	1P18	0900		Blackpool N.	47.440 87.008 86.235
1F11	0750		Liverpool L.S.	86.237 86.409					
1G21	0810	SX	Birmingham N.S.	87.009	1G23	0910	SX	Birmingham N.S.	87.001
1F14	0810	SUN	Liverpool L.S.	47.473 87.051	1B01	0925		Northampton	86.210 86.247
1H06	0820		Manchester P.	87.012	1D43	0930		Holyhead	47.434 86.219 86.407
1G22	0840	SX	Wolverhampton	86.206					

Train	Time	Days	Destination	Locos
1H30	0930	SUN	Manchester P.	47.470
1H30	0930	SUN	Manchester P.	87.037
1G24	0940		Wolverhampton	87.004 86.242
1J32	0940	SUN	Shrewsbury	47.457 86.275
1F14	0945		Liverpool L.S.	86.231 87.026
1S74	1000		Stranraer Hbr.	47.593 86.227
1P02	1000	SUN	Preston	47.467 86.448
1G25	1010	SX	Birmingham N.S.	86.408
1H08	1020		Manchester P.	86.412
1S57	1030		Glasgow C.	87.025
1G26	1040		Wolverhampton	86.215 87.004
1G26	1040	SUN	Wolverhampton	86.250
1F19	1050	SUN	Liverpool L.S.	47.456 86.444
1B02	1100	SX	Northampton	86.224
1G27	1110	SX	Birmingham N.S.	86.211
1B02	1110	SO	Northampton	86.426
1F22	1120		Liverpool L.S.	87.002
1D48	1130		Holyhead	47.433 86.207 86.246
1H32	1130	SUN	Manchester P.	47.477 86.260
1J25	1140		Shrewsbury	47.453 86.203 47.429 86.202
1G28	1140	SUN	Wolverhampton	87.054
1H11	1150		Manchester P.	86.218 87.013
1P62	1200		Blackpool N.	47.441 86.202 47.438 86.232
1P18	1200	SUN	Blackpool N.	47.526 86.445
1P18	1200	SUN	Preston	86.445
1G29	1210	SX	Birmingham N.S.	87.017
1F26	1220	SX	Liverpool L.S.	86.401
1G30	1240		Wolverhampton	86.201 87.017
1G05	1240	SUN	Wolverhampton	86.265
1H10	1250	SX	Manchester P.	86.403
1F26	1250	SO	Liverpool L.S.	86.422
1F28	1250	SUN	Liverpool L.S.	87.045
1S80	1300		Glasgow C.	86.406 87.028
1S63	1300	SUN	Glasgow C.	87.034
1G31	1310	SX	Birmingham N.S.	86.210
1F29	1320	FO	Liverpool L.S.	86.411
1H10	1320	SO	Manchester P.	86.247
1B03	1325	SX	Northampton	86.225
1H33	1330	SUN	Manchester P.	86.256
1G32	1340		Wolverhampton	87.005 86.201
1F33	1350	FSX	Liverpool L.S.	86.411
1S69	1400		Glasgow C.	87.001 87.005
1H34	1400	SUN	Manchester P.	86.269
2G33	1410	SX	Birmingham N.S.	86.223
1H12	1420	SX	Manchester P.	87.013
1F33	1420	SO	Liverpool L.S.	86.408
1F33	1430	FO	Liverpool L.S.	86.419
1P63	1430	SUN	Blackpool N.	47.483 86.439
1G34	1440		Wolverhampton	86.206 86.428
1F33	1450	SUN	Liverpool L.S.	86.266
1H12	1500	SO	Manchester P.	87.022
1G34	1500	SUN	Wolverhampton	86.268
1G35	1510	SX	Wolverhampton	87.022
1H13	1520		Manchester P.	87.009
1H39	1520	SUN	Manchester P.	86.441
1S83	1530		Glasgow C.	86.408 87.032
1S75	1530	SUN	Glasgow C.	87.050
1J33	1540	SX	Aberystwyth	37.401 47.543 86.216
1J33	1540	SO	Shrewsbury	47.429 86.425
1F35	1550		Liverpool L.S.	86.420 86.216
1H16	1600		Manchester P.	87.024 86.206
1G37	1610	SX	Birmingham N.S.	87.015
1H37	1610	SUN	Manchester P.	86.443
1D66	1617		Holyhead	47.432
1D66	1617		Holyhead	86.220
1D66	1617		Holyhead	87.007
1F40	1620	SUN	Liverpool L.S.	86.270
1P38	1630		Blackpool N.	47.440 86.224
1P38	1630	SUN	Barrow in Furness	47.526 87.055
1G38	1640		Wolverhampton	86.213 86.204
1F40	1650	SX	Liverpool L.S.	87.006
1B03	1650	SO	Northampton	86.426
1H43	1650	SUN	Manchester P.	86.435
1H20	1700		Manchester P.	87.023 87.006
1D60	1700	SUN	Holyhead	47.469 87.044
1J37	1710	SX	Shrewsbury	47.453 86.404
1F40	1710	SO	Liverpool L.S.	86.244
1J34	1710	SUN	Shrewsbury	47.457 86.262
1B06	1714	SX	Northampton	86.209
1B07	1720	SX	Bletchley	86.211
1S89	1730		Glasgow C.	87.020
1S89	1730	SUN	Glasgow C.	87.035
1F42	1735	FO	Liverpool L.S.	86.405 86.409
1K09	1735	FSX	Crewe	86.409
1K06	1735	SO	Crewe	86.240
1H25	1740	SX	Manchester P.	87.004
1J37	1740	SO	Shrewsbury	47.545 86.237
1B08	1745	SX	Northampton	86.221
1F47	1750	SX	Liverpool L.S.	86.215
1H21	1800		Manchester P.	86.208 86.424
1F45	1800	SUN	Liverpool L.S.	86.430
1G41	1810	SX	Wolverhampton	86.225
1B06	1810	SO	Northampton	86.427
1G38	1810	SUN	Wolverhampton	86.275
1B09	1814	SX	Northampton	86.228
1H19	1820	FO	Manchester P.	86.418
1F47	1820	SO	Liverpool L.S.	87.004
1H40	1820	SUN	Manchester P.	86.267
1P79	1825		Carlisle	87.001 87.011
1P79	1830	SUN	Carlisle	86.447
1G43	1840		Wolverhampton	86.210 86.208
1G43	1840	SUN	Wolverhampton	86.250
1G07	1843	FO	Wolverhampton	86.412
1D71	1850		Holyhead	47.434 87.017 86.246
1F43	1850	SUN	Liverpool L.S.	86.440
1H22	1900		Manchester P.	86.410 86.415
1D73	1900	SUN	Holyhead	47.466 87.040
1G44	1910	SX	Wolverhampton	87.008
1G44	1910	SUN	Wolverhampton	86.433
1F62	1920	SX	Liverpool L.S.	86.207
1H22	1920	SO	Manchester P.	87.026
1H36	1920	SUN	Manchester P.	86.438
1P49	1930		Blackpool N.	47.443 86.223 87.017
1P49	1930	SUN	Blackpool N.	47.478 86.260
1F61	1935	FO	Liverpool L.S.	85.002
1J44	1940		Shrewsbury	47.453 86.203 47.429 87.029
1G45	1940	SUN	Wolverhampton	87.037
1B10	1945	SX	Northampton	86.201
1F62	1950	SO	Liverpool L.S.	86.235
1F62	1950	SUN	Liverpool L.S.	86.444
1H23	2000	SX	Manchester P.	86.205
1G46	2010	SX	Wolverhampton	87.005
1B10	2010	SO	Northampton	86.233
1J36	2010	SUN	Shrewsbury	46.457 87.047
1H42	2020	SUN	Manchester P.	86.255
1H23	2028	SO	Manchester P.	86.202
1F63	2030	SX	Liverpool L.S.	86.218
1G46	2045	SO	Wolverhampton	86.426
1H24	2050	SX	Manchester P.	86.214
1F63	2050	SO	Liverpool L.S.	86.242
1F56	2050	SUN	Liverpool L.S.	86.251
1S07	2055	SX	Fort William	37.407 37.414 87.002
1S07	2055	SO	Inverness	87.033 47.600
1S07	2055	SUN	Inverness	87.049 37.407 37.414
1S06	2105	SX	Stranraer Hbr.	47.591 86.217
1S06	2105	SUN	Stranraer Hbr.	87.036 47.591
1G47	2110	SX	Wolverhampton	86.219
1G46	2110	SUN	Wolverhampton	86.265
1G47	2140	SUN	Wolverhampton	86.274

1D84	2150	SO	Holyhead	87.030 47.468
1H45	2150	SUN	Manchester P.	86.252
1D84	2200		Holyhead	47.432 86.231
1S18	2200	SO	Glasgow C.	87.031
1D84	2200	SUN	Holyhead	47.432 87.046
1G48	2210		Wolverhampton	86.227 86.217
1H46	2210	SUN	Manchester P.	87.054
1S25	2230		Inverness	47.590 87.018
				47.517 87.038
1S77	2240	SO	Edinburgh	87.002 47.528
1G48	2240	SUN	Wolverhampton	87.041
1S18	2300	SX	Glasgow C.	47.509 87.012
1S18	2300	SUN	Glasgow C.	87.042 47.509
1S26	2330	SX	Glasgow C.	87.015
1S26	2330	SUN	Glasgow C.	87.051
1G51	2340		Wolverhampton	86.229 86.206
1G49	2340	SUN	Wolverhampton	86.268
1S77	2345	SX	Edinburgh	47.505 87.009
1S77	2345	SUN	Edinburgh	87.039 47.505
1F53	2350	7	Liverpool L.S.	87.019 86.411
				86.213 86.407
				86.411 47.407
				86.256

Exeter St. D.

1O11	0550	SX	Waterloo	50.015
1O98	0550	SO	Hove	33.019
1O12	0642		Waterloo	50.018
2C68	0702		Penzance	50.024
2C08	0750		Paignton	50.023
1O14	0811	SX	Waterloo	50.020
1O14	0817	SO	Waterloo	50.020
1A28	0845	SUN	Paddington	50.036
1O15	0925	SUN	Waterloo	50.040
1O15	0936	SO	Waterloo	50.031
1O15	0938	SX	Waterloo	50.017
1O38	1105	SX	Portsmouth Hbr.	50.014
1O86	1105	SO	Brighton	47.565
1O18	1218		Waterloo	50.021
1O18	1225	SUN	Waterloo	50.044
2C15	1325		Paignton	50.023
1O19	1417		Waterloo	50.016
1O19	1420	SUN	Waterloo	50.041
1O21	1555	SUN	Waterloo	50.039
1O21	1607	SUN	Waterloo	50.039
1O21	1618		Waterloo	50.015
2C19	1725	SX	Paignton	47.538
1O22	1725	SUN	Waterloo	50.051
1O22	1733	SX	Waterloo	50.018
1O22	1745	SUN	Waterloo	50.051
1O23	1817	SO	Waterloo	50.018
1O23	1825	SUN	Waterloo	50.052
1O24	1947	SX	Waterloo	50.020
2O96	2025	SO	Basingstoke	50.034
2O96	2105	SUN	Salisbury	50.040
2C27	2151		Newton Abbot	50.021 50.031

Fareham

2T10	0624		Eastleigh	33.016

Fort William

1Y51	1005	MFSX	Mallaig	37.412
2Y51	1005		Mallaig	37.413
2Y53	1405		Mallaig	37.407
1T34	1415		Glasgow Q.S.	37.410
2Y55	1610		Mallaig	37.412 37.411
1M16	1740		Euston	87.001 37.407
				37.413
1M16	1740	SUN	Euston	37.415 37.417
				37.419
2Y57	2105		Mallaig	37.412 37.411

Gatwick Airport

2D25	0105	7	Victoria	73.104
1D67	0620	7	Victoria	73.101
1D69	0635	7	Victoria	73.102
1D71	0650	7	Victoria	73.103
1D73	0705	7	Victoria	73.104
1D75	0720	7	Victoria	73.105
1D77	0735	7	Victoria	73.106
1D79	0750	7	Victoria	73.107
1D81	0805	7	Victoria	73.101
1D83	0820	7	Victoria	73.102
1D85	0835	7	Victoria	73.103
1D87	0850	7	Victoria	73.104
1D89	0905	7	Victoria	73.105
1D91	0920	7	Victoria	73.106
1D93	0935	7	Victoria	73.107
1D95	0950	7	Victoria	73.101
1D01	1005	7	Victoria	73.102
1D03	1020	7	Victoria	73.103
1D05	1035	7	Victoria	73.104
1D07	1050	7	Victoria	73.105
1D09	1105	7	Victoria	73.106
1D11	1120	7	Victoria	73.107
1D13	1135	7	Victoria	73.101
1D15	1150	7	Victoria	73.102
1D17	1205	7	Victoria	73.103
1D19	1220	7	Victoria	73.104
1D21	1235	7	Victoria	73.105
1D23	1250	7	Victoria	73.106
1D25	1305	7	Victoria	73.107
1D27	1320	7	Victoria	73.101
1D29	1335	7	Victoria	73.102
1D31	1350	7	Victoria	73.103
1D33	1405	7	Victoria	73.104
1D35	1420	7	Victoria	73.105
1D37	1435	7	Victoria	73.106
1D39	1450	7	Victoria	73.107
1D41	1505	7	Victoria	73.101
1D43	1520	7	Victoria	73.102
1D45	1535	7	Victoria	73.103
1D47	1550	7	Victoria	73.104
1D49	1605	7	Victoria	73.105
1D51	1620	7	Victoria	73.106
1D53	1635	7	Victoria	73.107
1D55	1650	7	Victoria	73.101
1D57	1705	7	Victoria	73.102
1D59	1720	7	Victoria	73.103
1D61	1735	7	Victoria	73.104
1D63	1750	7	Victoria	73.105
1D65	1805	7	Victoria	73.106
1D67	1820	7	Victoria	73.107
1D69	1835	7	Victoria	73.101
1D71	1850	7	Victoria	73.102
1D73	1905	7	Victoria	73.103
1D75	1920	7	Victoria	73.104
1D77	1935	7	Victoria	73.105
1D79	1950	7	Victoria	73.106
1D81	2005	7	Victoria	73.107
1D83	2020	7	Victoria	73.101
1D85	2035	7	Victoria	73.102
1D87	2050	7	Victoria	73.103
1D89	2105	7	Victoria	73.104
1D91	2120	7	Victoria	73.105
1D93	2135	7	Victoria	73.106
1D95	2150	7	Victoria	73.107

1D01	2205	7	Victoria	73.101
1D03	2220	7	Victoria	73.102
1D05	2235	7	Victoria	73.103
1D09	2320	7	Victoria	73.104
1D13	2335		Victoria	73.106
1D17	2350	7	Victoria	73.101

Georgemas Jn.

2H71	1034	Thurso	37.421
2H73	1534	Thurso	37.421
2H75	2134	Thurso	37.421

Glasgow C.

1M18	0600		Euston	87.005	
1K03	0700		Ayr	87.003	86.248
1V59	0720		Penzance	47.537	86.212
				47.431	50.028
				87.027	
1M01	0740		Carlisle	47.506	
1M05	0810		Euston	86.228	87.020
1A01	0823		Stranraer Hbr.	47.509	
1O07	0850		Poole	47.448	87.010
1O07	0950	SUN	Poole	47.417	47.519
				47.665	
1M02	1013		Carlisle	47.593	
1V73	1050		Plymouth	47.447	87.003
				86.248	
1E31	1145		Harwich P.Q.	86.117	47.542
				47.542	
1B65	1150	SUN	Edinburgh	47.602	
1M34	1210		Euston	87.018	87.029
1A03	1223		Stranraer Hbr.	47.510	47.596
1M03	1345		Carlisle	47.594	
1M35	1410		Euston	86.214	87.031
1M19	1410	SUN	Euston	87.041	
1M56	1445	SUN	Carlisle	47.603	
1A03	1537	SUN	Stranraer Hbr.	47.660	
1M89	1545		Carlisle	47.506	
1M87	1550		Manchester V.	47.438	86.417
				86.238	
1M46	1610	SUN	Euston	87.042	
1M52	1710		Euston	87.016	
1M52	1710	SUN	Euston	87.039	
1V98	1720	SUN	Bristol T.M.	47.463	87.053
1M56	1730		Carlisle	47.592	47.597
1M01	1745	SUN	Carlisle	47.527	
1M47	1750		Birmingham N.S.	86.226	87.025
1M40	1850	SO	Manchester V.	47.437	86.118
1M40	1920	SX	Manchester V.	47.437	86.118
1M55	1945	SUN	Manchester V.	47.483	86.257
1A05	2153		Stranraer Hbr.	47.509	
1M10	2215	7	Euston	47.582	47.594
				87.012	47.598
				86.444	
1M11	2310	SX	Euston	87.010	
1V32	2310	SO	Bristol T.M.	47.510	47.467
				47.571	87.044
1M11	2310	SUN	Euston	87.043	
1V32	2350	SX	Plymouth	47.539	87.001
1V32	2350	SUN	Plymouth	47.539	87.048

Glasgow Q.S.

1O04	0655		Edinburgh	47.704	
1A51	0725	SX	Aberdeen	47.705	
1A53	0725	SO	Aberdeen	47.705	
1O08	0800		Edinburgh	47.703	
1O70	0800	SUN	Edinburgh	47.717	
1Y11	0820		Oban	37.408	
1O10	0830		Edinburgh	47.702	
1O12	0900		Edinburgh	47.704	
1O72	0900	SUN	Edinburgh	47.720	
1A57	0925		Aberdeen	47.707	
1A81	0925	SUN	Aberdeen	47.711	
1O14	0930		Edinburgh	47.701	
1H09	0933		Inverness	47.501	
1Y21	0950		Fort William	37.411	
1O16	1000		Edinburgh	47.703	
1O18	1030		Edinburgh	47.702	
1O20	1100		Edinburgh	47.704	
1O74	1100	SUN	Edinburgh	47.717	
1A59	1125		Aberdeen	47.708	
1A85	1125	SUN	Aberdeen	47.713	
1O22	1130		Edinburgh	47.701	
1O24	1200		Edinburgh	47.703	
1O76	1200	SUN	Edinburgh	47.720	
1Y13	1220		Oban	37.409	
1O26	1230		Edinburgh	47.702	
1O28	1300		Edinburgh	47.704	
1O78	1300	SUN	Edinburgh	47.719	
1A61	1325		Aberdeen	47.709	
1O30	1330		Edinburgh	47.701	
1H13	1333		Inverness	47.500	47.587
1O32	1400		Edinburgh	47.703	
1O80	1400	SUN	Edinburgh	47.717	
1O34	1430		Edinburgh	47.705	
1O36	1500		Edinburgh	47.710	
1O82	1500	SUN	Edinburgh	47.720	
1A63	1525		Dyce	47.702	
1A87	1525	SUN	Aberdeen	47.716	
1O38	1530		Edinburgh	47.704	
1L37	1555		Arbroath	47.515	
1O40	1600		Edinburgh	47.701	
1O84	1600	SUN	Edinburgh	47.719	
1O42	1630		Edinburgh	47.705	
1H51	1655	SUN	Inverness	47.523	
1O44	1700		Edinburgh	47.703	
1O86	1700	SUN	Edinburgh	47.717	
2O72	1714	SX	Edinburgh	47.587	
1A67	1725		Aberdeen	47.706	
1A91	1725	SUN	Aberdeen	47.714	
1O46	1730		Edinburgh	47.704	
1Y29	1750	SUN	Fort William	37.416	
1O48	1800		Edinburgh	47.701	
1O14	1800	SUN	Edinburgh	47.720	
1H15	1803		Inverness	47.503	47.517
1Y15	1820	SX	Oban	37.408	
1Y17	1820	SO	Oban	37.408	
1O50	1830		Edinburgh	47.705	
1O02	1830	SUN	Edinburgh	47.719	
1O52	1900		Edinburgh	47.703	
1O52	1900	SUN	Edinburgh	47.717	
1A71	1925		Aberdeen	47.708	
1A93	1925	SUN	Aberdeen	47.712	
1O54	1930		Edinburgh	47.704	
1O06	1930	SUN	Edinburgh	47.718	
1O56	2000		Edinburgh	47.701	
1O56	2000	SUN	Edinburgh	47.720	
1L51	2025		Dundee	47.709	
1O58	2030		Edinburgh	47.705	
1O68	2030	SUN	Edinburgh	47.719	
1O60	2100		Edinburgh	47.703	
1O60	2100	SUN	Edinburgh	47.717	
1L81	2125	SUN	Dundee	47.713	
1O62	2130		Edinburgh	47.704	
1O98	2130	SUN	Edinburgh	47.718	
1O64	2200		Edinburgh	47.701	
1O96	2200	SUN	Edinburgh	47.720	
1O66	2230		Edinburgh	47.705	
1O68	2300	SO	Edinburgh	47.703	
1L31	2330		Perth	47.702	47.592
1L31	2330	SUN	Perth	47.711	

Guildford

2P18	0710	SUN	Woking	73.123					

Harwich P.Q.

1M87	0720		Manchester P.	47.444		1M12	1320		Blackpool N.	31.405	47.445
1M86	0720		Manchester P.	47.445		1M51	1330	SUN	Birmingham N.S.	47.418	86.132
1A63	0725	SUN	Liverpool St.	86.131		1M80	1705		Wolverhampton	31.402	
1A63	0745	SX	Liverpool St.	86.112		1A67	1840	SX	Liverpool St.	86.104	
1S85	0750		Edinburgh	47.533	86.118	1C47	1840	SO	Liverpool St.	86.116	
1A63	0750	SO	Liverpool St.	86.108		1A67	1840	SUN	Liverpool St.	86.121	
1A35	1315	SUN	Liverpool St.	47.425							

Hereford

1A10	0604	SX	Paddington	47.540		1A67	1615	SUN	Paddington	50.045
1A28	0808	SO	Paddington	47.561		1A80	1825	SUN	Paddington	50.038

Holyhead

1A04	0045	SUN	Euston	47.465	86.449	1A27	1305	SUN	Euston	47.469 86.255
				87.037	87.037	1A52	1352	SUN	Euston	47.466 86.436
1A04	0115		Euston	47.435	87.019					86.445
1V03	0515		Cardiff C.	47.435	47.558	1V13	1410	SUN	Cardiff C.	47.584
1A25	0605		Euston	47.432	87.017	1A78	1615		Euston	47.434 86.407
1V05	0714		Cardiff C.	47.434	47.558	1A39	1656	SUN	Euston	47.465 86.249
1A45	0856		Euston	47.433	87.020					86.432
				87.009		1G56	1710		Birmingham N.S.	47.433 86.220
1A52	1255		Euston	47.432	86.207					87.007
				86.246						

Honiton

1O15	0949	SUN	Waterloo	50.040		1O19	1446	SUN	Waterloo	50.041
1O18	1249	SUN	Waterloo	50.044		1O21	1619	SUN	Waterloo	50.039

Hull

1A20	1505	SX	King's Cross	47.651	

Huntly

1A56	1820		Aberdeen	47.650	

Inverness

1A42	0500		Aberdeen	47.503		1B36	1700		Edinburgh	47.514
1A40	0600		Aberdeen	47.504		1B76	1730	SUN	Edinburgh	47.530
2H61	0635		Wick	37.424		2H65	1735		Wick	37.422
2H81	0655		Kyle of Lochalsh	37.422		2H85	1755		Kyle of Lochalsh	37.424
1A46	0832		Aberdeen	47.514		1A58	1800		Aberdeen	47.502
1T36	0840		Glasgow Q.S.	47.515		1T42	1820		Glasgow Q.S.	47.505
2H83	1015		Kyle of Lochalsh	37.426		1A88	1840	SUN	Aberdeen	47.524
1M42	1030		Euston	47.595	87.019	1D32	1930	SX	Mossend Yard	47.590
				47.589		1M16	1930	SO	Euston	47.587 47.465
1A48	1032		Aberdeen	47.590	47.503					86.445
2H63	1135		Wick	37.423		1D34	1930	SUN	Mossend Yard	47.600
1T30	1225		Glasgow Q.S.	47.503	47.517	1A60	2055		Aberdeen	47.512 47.503
1A50	1232		Aberdeen	47.657		1M15	2100	SX	Euston	47.588 47.599
1B34	1430		Edinburgh	47.501						86.403 86.407
1A52	1432		Aberdeen	47.512		1T04	2340	SX	Glasgow Q.S.	47.500
1A86	1540	SUN	Aberdeen	47.522		1T04	2340	SUN	Glasgow Q.S.	47.520
1T88	1650	SUN	Glasgow Q.S.	47.525						

Inverurie

2A78	0733	SX	Aberdeen	47.513	

Ipswich

1P03	0540	SX	Liverpool St.	86.105		1M70	0928		Birmingham N.S.	31.424
2P01	0550	SUN	Liverpool St.	86.122		1M66	1322	SUN	Birmingham N.S.	31.429
1P14	0730		Norwich	86.111		1E71	1602		Sheffield	31.451

Kensington O.

1O28	1033	SUN	Dover W.D.	47.575		2O87	1703	SX	Clapham Jn.	33.106
2O85	1612	SX	Clapham Jn.	33.106		2O88	1727	SX	Clapham Jn.	33.106
2O86	1637	SX	Clapham Jn.	33.106						

King's Cross

1D01	1033	SX	Hull	47.651		1L07	1210	SUN	Leeds	47.666
1L06	1110	SUN	Leeds	47.662		1N20	1910	FO	Newcastle	47.652

1S70 2038 7 Aberdeen 47.656 | 1S29 2359 SX Edinburgh 47.653
1S79 2215 SX Aberdeen 47.658 | 1S29 2359 SUN Edinburgh 47.653
1S79 2215 SUN Aberdeen 47.659

King's Lynn

1H13 0650 SO Liverpool St. 31.420 86.103 | 1H29 1500 Liverpool St. 47.420 86.103
1H15 0745 Liverpool St. 47.420 86.108 | 1H27 1500 SUN Liverpool St. 47.423 86.124
47.420 86.102 | 1H33 1700 SO Liverpool St. 47.421 86.104
2HO1 0800 SUN Cambridge 47.424 | 1H31 1730 SUN Liverpool St. 47.424 86.120
1H17 0900 Liverpool St. 47.421 86.104 | 1H33 1735 SX Liverpool St. 47.421 86.106
1H21 1100 Liverpool St. 47.420 86.103 | 1H37 1905 SX Liverpool St. 47.420 86.103
1H25 1300 Liverpool St. 47.421 86.104 | 1H37 1940 SO Liverpool St. 47.420 86.107
1H23 1300 SUN Liverpool St. 47.424 86.126 | 1H35 1950 SUN Liverpool St. 47.423 86.126

Kirkcaldy

2K04 0730 SX Edinburgh 47.706

Kyle of Lochalsh

2H80 0710 Inverness 37.425 | 2H84 1710 Inverness 37.426
2H82 1130 Inverness 37.422

Lancaster

1A61 1330 Euston 86.208

Leamington Spa

1V10 0651 SX Paddington 50.010

Leeds

1M27 0604 SO Carlisle 47.642 | 1A23 1545 SUN King's Cross 47.662
1M09 0842 Carlisle 47.508 | 1M72 1625 Carlisle 47.508
1M45 1027 Nottingham 45.101 | 1M66 1627 Nottingham 45.101
1M43 1042 Carlisle 47.507 | 1A25 1648 SUN King's Cross 47.666
1M61 1321 Carlisle 47.642

Leicester

1E26 2210 Sheffield 45.101

Liverpool L.S.

1K07 0015 Stafford 86.201 | 1A32 1150 Euston 86.418 86.204
1K07 0015 SUN Stafford 47.407 86.270 | 1A19 1159 SUN Euston 47.456 87.040
1A08 0625 Euston 86.202 | 1E43 1245 Sheffield 31.406
1E25 0630 Sheffield 31.406 | 1E29 1252 SUN Sheffield 31.414
1E00 0703 Newcastle 47.404 | 1O46 1302 SUN Poole 47.484
1A11 0705 SX Euston 86.411 | 1E99 1303 Newcastle 47.401
1O66 0720 Brighton 47.534 86.217 | 1A37 1315 Euston 86.409 86.237
1E29 0738 Sheffield 31.410 | 1O46 1319 SUN Poole 47.484
1A07 0740 SUN Euston 47.456 86.272 | 1E68 1345 Sheffield 31.410
87.050 | 1E99 1350 SUN Newcastle 47.409
1A11 0743 SO Euston 86.422 | 1V81 1405 SUN Paddington 47.577
1A07 0755 SUN Euston 47.456 87.050 | 1O08 1410 Poole 47.450 47.536
1A19 0820 Euston 86.401 86.236 | 47.452
1A09 0835 SUN Euston 47.473 86.441 | 1V81 1417 SUN Paddington 47.577
1E42 0845 Sheffield 31.407 | 1E30 1422 SUN Sheffield 31.415
1A09 0845 SUN Euston 47.473 86.441 | 1A24 1429 SUN Euston 47.474 86.444
1E06 0850 SUN Newcastle 47.407 | 47.474 86.444
1O06 0855 SUN Southampton C. 47.568 | 1E46 1445 Sheffield 31.407
1E82 0903 Newcastle 47.403 | 1A51 1500 Euston 86.205 87.026
1O06 0910 SUN Southampton C. 47.568 | 1E19 1503 Newcastle 47.405
1G16 0920 Birmingham N.S. 86.205 86.245 | 1A44 1535 SUN Euston 86.251
1A13 0938 SUN Euston 47.470 86.435 | 1E47 1545 Cleethorpes 31.411
1E44 0945 Sheffield 31.411 | 1E16 1550 SUN Newcastle 47.412
1A27 0950 Euston 86.209 86.428 | 1E23 1552 SUN Sheffield 31.412
1A13 0958 SUN Euston 47.470 86.435 | 1A64 1605 Euston 87.002
1O96 1030 Dover W.D. 47.535 86.222 | 1A29 1610 SUN Euston 86.434
1G02 1037 SUN Birmingham N.S. 47.474 86.440 | 1O09 1615 Poole 47.446 47.439
1G02 1042 SUN Birmingham N.S. 47.474 86.440 | 1E52 1645 Sheffield 31.409
1E85 1045 Yarmouth 31.408 31.421 | 1A76 1650 FO Euston 86.217
31.404 | 1A34 1700 SUN Euston 86.274 86.450
1E28 1048 SUN Newcastle 47.408 | 1E16 1703 Newcastle 47.406
1E26 1052 SUN Sheffield 31.416 | 1A76 1705 FX Euston 86.217
1E08 1103 Newcastle 47.402 | 1G08 1715 SUN Birmingham N.S. 87.052
1G17 1130 Birmingham Int. 86.204 86.423 | 1E18 1742 SUN Newcastle 47.411
1E34 1145 Sheffield 31.401 | 1E57 1745 Sheffield 31.401
1A19 1146 SUN Euston 47.456 87.040 | 1A81 1752 FO Euston 86.231

Train	Time	Days	Destination	Ref	Ref
1E34	1752	SUN	Cleethorpes	31.417	
1A76	1805	SO	Euston	86.217	
1A85	1815	SX	Euston	86.419	86.231
1A42	1815	SUN	Euston	87.046	
1E64	1845		Sheffield	31.406	
1E35	1852	SUN	Sheffield	31.413	
1E93	1858		Newcastle	47.404	
1G62	1900		Birmingham N.S.	86.222	86.245
1A70	1920	SX	Euston	87.012	
1A79	1920	SO	Euston	86.222	
1V99	1920	SUN	Paddington	47.572	86.254
1A45	1930	SUN	Euston	86.258	87.045
1E31	1942	SUN	Newcastle	47.410	
1E53	1945	SX	Sheffield	31.410	
1E37	1952	SUN	Sheffield	31.416	
1A42	2020	FO	Euston	86.414	
1E38	2052	SUN	Sheffield	31.414	
1E54	2145		Sheffield	31.407	

Liverpool St.

Train	Time	Days	Destination	Ref	Ref
1H04	0423		Cambridge	86.107	
1P08	0435		Ipswich	86.111	
1P18	0720		Norwich	96.113	
1P24	0830		Norwich	86.105	86.116
1P12	0830	SUN	Yarmouth	86.128	
1H06	0835		King's Lynn	47.420	86.104
1P12	0900	SUN	Norwich	47.427	
1A66	0920	SUN	Harwich P.Q.	47.425	86.122
1P28	0930		Norwich	86.109	
1H08	0935		Cambridge	86.107	
1H08	0935	SUN	King's Lynn	47.424	86.120
1A66	0940		Harwich P.Q.	86.106	
1P32	1030		Norwich	86.114	
1P14	1030	SUN	Norwich	86.131	
1H10	1035		King's Lynn	47.421	86.103
1P38	1130	SX	Norwich	86.101	
1P40	1130	SO	Norwich	86.101	
1H12	1135		Cambridge	86.102	
1P42	1230		Norwich	86.115	
1P18	1230	SUN	Norwich	86.130	
1H14	1235		King's Lynn	47.420	86.104
1P46	1330		Norwich	86.111	
1H16	1335		Cambridge	86.107	
1P48	1430		Norwich	86.113	
1P24	1430	SUN	Norwich	86.119	
1H18	1435		King's Lynn	47.421	86.103
1H18	1435	SUN	King's Lynn	47.424	86.124
1P52	1530		Norwich	86.105	
1H20	1535		Cambridge	86.102	
1A42	1620	SX	Harwich P.Q.	86.104	
1P56	1630		Norwich	86.109	
1P28	1630	SUN	Norwich	86.123	
1H22	1635		King's Lynn	47.420	86.106
				47.420	86.104
1H22	1635	SUN	King's Lynn	47.423	86.120
1P58	1700		Norwich	86.114	86.114
1P32	1730	SUN	Norwich	86.128	
1H24	1735	SX	Cambridge	86.107	
1P66	1740	SX	Norwich	86.112	
1P72	1820	FO	Norwich	86.110	
1P74	1830		Norwich	86.101	
1P36	1830	SUN	Norwich	86.131	
1H26	1835		King's Lynn	47.421	86.103
				47.421	86.107
1H26	1835	SUN	King's Lynn	47.424	86.126
1P76	1930		Norwich	86.115	
1P38	1930	SUN	Norwich	86.130	
1H28	1935	SO	Cambridge	86.102	
1A62	1950		Harwich P.Q.	86.111	
1A62	1950	SUN	Harwich P.Q.	86.127	
1P78	2030		Norwich	86.108	
1P42	2030	SUN	Norwich	86.125	
1H30	2035	FO	King's Lynn	31.425	86.102
1H30	2035	FX	Cambridge	86.102	86.104
1H30	2035	SUN	Cambridge	86.124	
1P82	2130		Norwich	86.113	
1P44	2130	SUN	Norwich	86.119	
1H32	2135	SX	Cambridge	86.106	
1P84	2300	SO	Norwich	47.422	
1P84	2300	SUN	Norwich	86.129	
1H34	2305	SUN	Cambridge	86.120	

Llandudno Junction

Train	Time	Days	Destination	Ref	Ref
1A41	1300	SUN	Euston	47.462	87.051
1A41	1321	SUN	Euston	47.462	87.051

London Bridge

Train	Time	Days	Destination	Ref
1GO1	0245		Deal	73.116
1G03	0310		Sittingbourne	73.117
1R03	0330		Dover W.D.	73.115
1R03	0345	SUN	Dover W.D.	33.038
1G01	0409	SUN	Ramsgate	73.124

Mallaig

Train	Time	Days	Destination	Ref	Ref
2Y54	1220		Fort William	37.412	37.410
1T46	1550	SX	Fort William	37.407	
1T46	1550	SO	Glasgow Q.S.	37.407	
2Y58	1850		Fort William	37.412	37.411

Manchester P.

Train	Time	Days	Destination	Ref	Ref
1A01	0030		Euston	86.206	
1A01	0030	SUN	Euston	47.464	86.266
1V01	0042	MO	Cardiff C.	47.551	86.402
1060	0305		Brighton	47.436	47.535
				86.404	86.240
1K10	0615	SX	Stafford	86.204	
1A02	0620		Euston	86.408	
1A24	0705	SX	Euston	86.207	
1A21	0723		Euston	86.225	86.427
1O03	0730	SUN	Southampton C.	47.569	47.572
1A10	0735		Euston	87.015	86.246
1O29	0740		Dover W.D.	47.533	86.229
				87.030	
1A16	0805	SX	Euston	86.421	86.201
1O03	0808		Poole	47.450	
1A16	0820	SO	Euston	86.201	
1A11	0820	SUN	Euston	47.482	86.268
1A03	0850	SUN	Euston	47.480	86.270
1A29	0930		Euston	87.022	
1A22	0935	SUN	Euston	47.464	87.044
1A33	1030		Euston	87.024	87.007
1A16	1030	SUN	Euston	47.477	86.430
1V61	1117	SUN	Paddington	47.461	
1A43	1130	SX	Euston	86.216	
1A23	1130	SUN	Euston	47.472	86.433
1A43	1148	SO	Euston	86.216	
1O74	1155		Brighton	47.534	87.021
				86.230	
1A49	1300	SX	Euston	86.404	
1V78	1300	SUN	Penzance	47.480	47.570
1A21	1305	SUN	Euston	47.482	87.037
1G08	1326		Birmingham N.S.	87.012	86.241
1A49	1335	SO	Euston	86.240	
1K01	1401		Stafford	47.541	
1V07	1412		Cardiff C.	47.550	
1A26	1418	SUN	Euston	47.470	86.260

1A59 1430 SX	Euston	87.011	
1A38 1455 FSO	Euston	86.412	
1E87 1527	Harwich P.Q.	47.444	
1O90 1539 SUN	Brighton	47.566 87.038	
1A30 1555 SUN	Euston	87.047	
1A66 1600 SX	Euston	86.219	
1A67 1630	Euston	86.218 87.033	
1O90 1640	Brighton	47.533 86.416	
		86.412 87.012	
1A40 1650 SUN	Euston	87.049	
1A70 1740 SX	Euston	86.229	
1A77 1755 SUN	Euston	86.259	

1A70 1800 SO	Euston	87.030	
1A49 1800 SUN	Euston	86.446	
1G09 1806	Birmingham Int.	86.403 87.013	
1V15 1827 SUN	Cardiff C.	47.583	
1A77 1855	Euston	87.013 86.247	
1G00 1855 SUN	Birmingham N.S.	86.263	
1A43 1915 SUN	Euston	86.256	
1V19 1920	Paddington	47.539 86.204	
		47.430 87.022	
1A80 2000	Euston	87.009 86.206	
1G66 2140 SUN	Birmingham N.S.	86.269	

Manchester V.

2F25 0715	Liverpool L.S.	47.402	
1S45 0735	Glasgow C.	47.437 86.214	
		87.031	

1S49 1025	Glasgow C.	47.440 86.226	
1S49 1406 SUN	Glasgow C.	47.479 86.257	

Montrose

2A76 1837 SX	Aberdeen	47.657	

Mossend Yard

1H03 0322 SO	Inverness	47.595	

1H03 0327 SX	Inverness	47.595	

Newbury

1F07 0706 SX	Paddington	50.006	

Newcastle

1M53 0605	Liverpool L.S.	47.401	
1O05 0745	Poole	47.545 47.655	
		47.413 47.560	
1M63 0800 SUN	Liverpool L.S.	47.412	
1M58 0825	Liverpool L.S.	47.405	
1M65 1000 SUN	Liverpool L.S.	47.411	
1M63 1025	Liverpool L.S.	47.406	
1M67 1200 SUN	Liverpool L.S.	47.410	

1M26 1225	Liverpool L.S.	47.404	
1M76 1425	Liverpool L.S.	47.403	
1O09 1440 SUN	Poole	47.480 47.488	
1M71 1450 SUN	Liverpool L.S.	47.407	
1M32 1625	Liverpool L.S.	47.402	
1M75 1650 SUN	Liverpool L.S.	47.408	
1M19 1825	Liverpool L.S.	47.401	
1M80 1930 SUN	Liverpool L.S.	47.409	

Newton Abbot

2C31 0624 SX	Exeter St. D.	50.023	
2C06 0740	Paignton	50.014 47.565	

2C10 0940	Paignton	50.023	
2C45 1550 SX	Exeter St. D.	47.538	

Northampton

1A73 0715 SX	Euston	86.224	
1A30 0740	Euston	86.227 86.223	
1A83 0810 SX	Euston	86.215	
1A55 0902 SO	Euston	86.239	

1A22 1102	Euston	86.210 86.247	
1A35 1302	Euston	86.224 86.426	
1A53 1555	Euston	86.225 86.426	

Norwich

1P03 0440 SO	Liverpool St.	86.116	
1P05 0540	Liverpool St.	86.109 86.109	
1P07 0618 SX	Liverpool St.	86.106	
2P06 0630	Yarmouth	31.423 31.422	
1P03 0650 SUN	Colchester	47.426	
1P03 0650 SUN	Liverpool St.	47.428	
1P13 0655 SO	Liverpool St.	86.114	
1P03 0655 SUN	Liverpool St.	86.130	
2P08 0700 SX	Yarmouth	31.422	
1P13 0700 SX	Liverpool St.	86.114	
1P15 0725 SO	Liverpool St.	86.105	
1M68 0727	Birmingham N.S.	31.425	
1P15 0755 SX	Liverpool St.	86.102	
1P19 0755 SO	Liverpool St.	86.101	
1P19 0800 SX	Liverpool St.	86.101	
1P23 0855	Liverpool St.	86.115	
1P07 0855 SUN	Liverpool St.	86.119	
1P25 0955	Liverpool St.	86.111	
1P29 1055	Liverpool St.	86.113	
1P11 1055 SUN	Liverpool St.	86.121	
1M73 1127	Birmingham N.S.	31.423	
1P33 1155	Liverpool St.	86.105 86.116	

1P37 1255	Liverpool St.	86.109	
1P15 1255 SUN	Liverpool St.	86.128	
1E39 1310 SUN	Sheffield	31.418	
1M74 1327	Birmingham N.S.	31.422	
1P39 1355	Liverpool St.	86.114	
1P17 1355 SUN	Liverpool St.	86.131	
1P45 1455 SO	Liverpool St.	86.101	
1P45 1505 SX	Liverpool St.	86.101	
1P49 1555	Liverpool St.	86.115	
1P21 1555 SUN	Liverpool St.	86.130	
1M68 1635 SUN	Birmingham N.S.	31.419	
1M77 1640	Birmingham N.S.	31.403 31.426	
1P53 1655	Liverpool St.	86.111	
1P23 1655 SUN	Liverpool St.	86.127	
1P55 1755	Liverpool St.	86.113	
1P27 1755 SUN	Liverpool St.	86.119	
1P59 1855	Liverpool St.	86.105	
1P33 1855 SUN	Liverpool St.	86.129	
1P63 2025	Liverpool St.	86.109	
1P35 2025 SUN	Liverpool St.	86.128	
2P39 2255 SUN	Ipswich	31.428	

Nottingham

1C06 0603 SX	St. Pancras	47.451	
1M22 0718	Blackpool N.	47.640	

1E31 0725 SX	Leeds	45.101	
1E31 0742 SO	Leeds	45.101	

1E41	1325		Leeds	45.101	2F25	1854		Leicester	45.101
1M26	1544		Blackpool N.	47.641					

Oban

1T12	0800		Glasgow Q.S.	37.409	1T44	1800		Glasgow Q.S.	37.409
1T28	1300		Glasgow Q.S.	37.408	2Y92	1800	SUN	Crianlarich	37.418

Oxford

1F01	0628	SX	Paddington	50.008	1F33	1300		Paddington	50.008
1F05	0640	SX	Paddington	50.004	1F07	1325	SUN	Paddington	50.037
1F03	0654	SX	Paddington	50.002	1F35	1355		Paddington	50.010
1F13	0713	SX	Paddington	50.011	1F37	1600	SX	Paddington	50.011
1F11	0726	SX	Paddington	50.013	1F39	1600	SO	Paddington	50.004
1F13	0735	SO	Paddington	50.012	1F39	1655	SX	Paddington	50.008
1F19	0750	SX	Paddington	50.003	1F41	1655	SO	Paddington	50.008
1F01	0845	SUN	Paddington	50.049	1F09	1720	SUN	Paddington	50.049
1F27	0955		Paddington	50.001 50.030	1F41	1740	SX	Paddington	50.010
1F03	0955	SUN	Paddington	50.047	1F43	1912		Paddington	50.002 50.010
1F29	1055	SX	Paddington	50.005	1F45	2012		Paddington	50.005 50.013
1F20	1055	SO	Paddington	50.004	1F47	2108	SO	Paddington	50.030
1F33	1115	SUN	Paddington	50.038	1F11	2130	SUN	Paddington	50.036
1F31	1200		Paddington	50.011					

Paddington

1M09	0550		Liverpool L.S.	47.536	1M42	1752	SX	Wolverhampton	50.004
1M10	0703		Manchester P.	47.541	1M58	1752	SO	Birmingham N.S.	47.561
1F12	0817	SO	Oxford	50.030	1M61	1753	SX	Banbury	50.011
1F12	0820	SX	Oxford	50.001	1F40	1754	SX	Twyford	50.001
1M08	0900	SUN	Wolverhampton	47.460	1B58	1807	FO	Swansea	47.549
1M20	0917		Birmingham N.S.	50.013	1F42	1810	SX	Newbury	50.013
1F12	1100	SUN	Oxford	50.037	1M18	1810	SUN	Manchester P.	47.461 86.271
1M17	1117		Birmingham N.S.	50.012	1B56	1812	SO	Hereford	50.035
1F14	1200	SUN	Oxford	50.046	1F44	1814	SX	Oxford	50.007
1F20	1217		Oxford	50.010	1F46	1816	SX	Twyford	50.006
1F22	1317		Oxford	50.004	1B56	1825	SUN	Hereford	47.573
1B33	1400	SUN	Hereford	50.038	1F50	1832	SX	Oxford	50.005
1F24	1417		Oxford	50.011	1C72	1902	FO	Bristol T.M.	50.029
1C53	1441	FO	Plymouth	47.548	1C73	1905	FO	Plymouth	47.547
1F26	1517		Oxford	50.008	1F52	1909		Oxford	50.012 50.030
1C60	1542	FO	Plymouth	47.546	1F54	1922	SX	Reading G.	50.008
1F18	1610	SUN	Oxford	50.048	1F56	2022		Oxford	50.003 50.004
1F30	1612	SX	Oxford	50.010	1M58	2022	SUN	Wolverhampton	47.576
1F30	1617	SO	Oxford	50.010	1C79	2045	SO	Exeter St. D.	50.010
1C63	1650	SUN	Bristol T.M.	50.053	1C06	2325	SO	Penzance	50.033 50.054
1B46	1702	SX	Hereford	47.540					50.054 50.054
1F32	1705		Didcot Parkway	50.003 50.013	1C07	2335	SO	Westbury	50.030
1F36	1727	SX	Westbury	50.009	1C02	2359	SX	Penzance	47.538 47.543
1F38	1730	SX	Oxford	50.002					47.543

Paignton

2C37	0817		Exeter St. D.	50.014 47.565	2C47	1640		Exeter St. D.	50.019 50.034
2C38	0855		Newton Abbot	50.023	1S19	1838		Glasgow C.	86.412 37.001
2C40	1025		Exeter St. D.	50.023					47.538 86.413
2C43	1430		Newton Abbot	50.023					

Penzance

2C83	0911		Plymouth	50.029 50.032	2C86	1525	SX	Plymouth	50.025
1S87	1027		Glasgow C.	47.538 47.539	1F88	1830		Bristol T.M.	50.024 50.028
				87.003 86.248					50.022
1S86	1040	SUN	Edinburgh	47.458 47.463	1A02	1920	SO	Paddington	47.562 50.032
				50.056	1A02	2135		Paddington	47.448 47.537
2C84	1214		Plymouth	50.024	1A02	2140	SUN	Paddington	50.057
1O22	1410	SUN	Waterloo	50.042					

Perth

1A41	0110		Aberdeen	47.708	2B52	0710		Edinburgh	47.710
1A95	0120	SUN	Aberdeen	47.601	1C87	2140	SX	Carstairs	47.504
1T04	0340		Stirling	47.511	1C87	2140	SUN	Carstairs	47.531
1A43	0625		Dyce	47.709					

Peterborough

2H27	2110		Cambridge	31.452

Petersfield

2P06	0600	SUN	Guildford	73.123

Plymouth

Train	Time	Days	Destination	Refs	
1S71	1028		Glasgow C.	87.010	47.543
1S71	1425	SUN	Glasgow C.	50.055	86.431
1A63	1437	FO	Paddington	50.029	
2C72	1520	FX	Penzance	50.024	50.032
2C74	1557		Penzance	50.022	
1F84	1621		Bristol T.M.	50.026	50.024
1A78	1730	SUN	Paddington	47.578	
1A87	1830	SUN	Paddington	47.579	
1S19	1840	SO	Glasgow C.	37.002	47.538
				87.029	
1S19	1840	SUN	Glasgow C.	47.521	47.521
				47.528	47.528
				47.582	

Poole

Train	Time	Days	Destination	Refs	
1M88	0625	SX	Manchester P.	47.446	
1M88	0633	SO	Manchester P.	47.446	
1W06	0735	SX	Waterloo	33.108	
1W06	0739	SUN	Waterloo	33.113	33.116
				73.119	
1W06	0741	SO	Waterloo	33.108	73.110
1S39	0834		Glasgow C.	87.027	47.447
				47.448	86.212
1M08	0932	SUN	Liverpool L.S.	47.471	
1E63	1038		Newcastle	47.449	47.447
				47.655	
1E63	1040	SO	Newcastle	47.447	47.455
1S39	1132	SUN	Aberdeen	47.481	
1M07	1238		Manchester P.	47.449	47.454
1M23	1458		Liverpool L.S.	47.450	47.454
				86.216	
1M40	1732		Liverpool L.S.	47.536	47.545
				86.204	47.452
				47.560	87.022
1M40	1732	SUN	Manchester P.	86.254	

Portsmouth Hbr.

Train	Time	Days	Destination	Refs	
2V56	0550		Cardiff C.	33.004	33.014
				33.002	47.556
2V58	0656		Cardiff C.	33.011	33.006
				33.002	
2H12	0723	SUN	Salisbury	33.026	
1V38	0810		Cardiff C.	33.003	33.011
2H18	0915	SUN	Salisbury	33.023	
1V46	0915	SUN	Bristol T.M.	33.033	
2H18	0915	SUN	Salisbury	33.037	
1V46	0915	SUN	Westbury	33.037	
2V57	0924	SUN	Westbury	33.023	
2V32	1003	SUN	Reading G.	33.115	
1V54	1010		Swansea	33.001	37.402
				47.563	
2V34	1103	SUN	Reading G.	33.110	
1V58	1110		Cardiff C.	33.006	33.012
				33.008	47.564
1V12	1203	SX	Paignton	50.019	
1V62	1210		Cardiff C.	33.009	33.012
				33.002	33.005
1V66	1310		Bristol T.M.	33.007	
1V70	1410		Cardiff C.	33.007	47.555
				33.006	
1V66	1415	SUN	Cardiff C.	33.023	33.024
2V39	1503	SUN	Reading G.	33.115	
1V77	1510		Bristol T.M.	33.004	33.020
1V77	1515	SUN	Cardiff C.	33.025	37.405
1P28	1530	SX	Waterloo	50.014	
2V41	1603	SUN	Reading G.	33.110	
1V79	1610		Cardiff C.	33.003	37.402
				47.563	
1V79	1615	SUN	Cardiff C.	33.025	33.037
1V85	1710		Cardiff C.	33.010	50.026
				33.007	33.014
1V87	1810		Cardiff C.	33.001	33.004
				33.003	
1V87	1815	SUN	Bristol T.M.	33.031	
1V92	1915	SUN	Cardiff C.	33.034	37.405
2V45	2003	SUN	Reading G.	33.115	
1V96	2015	SUN	Cardiff C.	33.026	33.027
1V96	2025		Cardiff C.	33.005	33.011
				33.010	50.024
1V96	2025	SO	Bristol T.M.	33.010	
1V96	2025	SO	Westbury	33.010	
2V46	2103	SUN	Reading G.	33.110	
2H62	2125		Salisbury	33.006	33.011
2H64	2242	SUN	Salisbury	33.030	

Preston

Train	Time	Days	Destination	Refs	
1A46	1341	SUN	Euston	47.467	86.429
1A46	1423	SUN	Euston	86.429	
1A47	1550	SUN	Euston	86.448	
1A51	1715	SUN	Euston	86.253	86.445
1P10	1940	SX	Barrow in Furness	47.441	
1P10	1950	SUN	Blackpool N.	47.478	
1J27	2053		Manchester V.	47.442	47.441

Reading G.

Train	Time	Days	Destination	Refs	
2C04	0600	SX	Oxford	50.011	
2O03	0750	SUN	Portsmouth Hbr.	33.114	33.115
2O04	0850	SUN	Portsmouth Hbr.	33.110	
2O08	1250	SUN	Portsmouth Hbr.	33.115	
2O09	1350	SUN	Portsmouth Hbr.	33.110	
2O14	1750	SUN	Portsmouth Hbr.	33.115	
2O16	1850	SUN	Portsmouth Hbr.	33.110	
2O21	2300	SUN	Basingstoke	33.115	

St. Pancras

Train	Time	Days	Destination	Refs
1D17	1620	SUN	Nottingham	47.487
1P13	1730	SX	Derby	47.451

Salisbury

Train	Time	Days	Destination	Refs	
2L06	0600	SO	Basingstoke	33.107	
2V05	0602	SO	Exeter St. D.	50.031	
2H03	0605		Portsmouth Hbr.	33.001	
2V54	0609	SX	Exeter St. D.	50.017	
1L00	0612	SX	Waterloo	33.105	
2L10	0640	SX	Waterloo	50.019	
1L00	0700	SO	Waterloo	50.015	
2T13	0702	SX	Eastleigh	33.007	
2T13	0703	SO	Eastleigh	33.017	
2L14	0716	SX	Waterloo	33.015	
1L02	0748		Waterloo	33.106	33.106
1L04	0825	SUN	Waterloo	50.043	
1L06	0944	SO	Waterloo	33.107	
1Y52	1017	SUN	Brighton	33.026	
2H23	1119	SUN	Portsmouth Hbr.	33.023	
1L08	1210	SO	Waterloo	33.106	
1L08	1315	SX	Waterloo	33.106	
2H31	1324	SUN	Portsmouth Hbr.	33.037	
2H35	1430	SUN	Portsmouth Hbr.	33.031	
1L10	1515	SX	Waterloo	33.107	
1L10	1532	SO	Waterloo	33.107	
2L40	1636	SX	Basingstoke	33.108	

1L12	1725	SX	Waterloo	33.015	1L12	1820	SUN	Waterloo	33.029
1L12	1732	SO	Waterloo	33.106	2L40	1920	SO	Basingstoke	33.021
1L12	1803	SUN	Waterloo	33.029	2L50	2120	SO	Basingstoke	33.107

Sheffield

1M29	0604		Liverpool L.S.	31.411	1M39	1522		Liverpool L.S.	31.406
1M72	0655	SX	Liverpool L.S.	31.408	1M20	1538	SUN	Liverpool L.S.	31.416
1M72	0722	SO	Liverpool L.S.	31.408	1M34	1622		Liverpool L.S.	31.410
1E88	0755		Ipswich	31.451	1M37	1700	SUN	Liverpool L.S.	31.414
1M23	0759	SUN	Liverpool L.S.	31.415	1M38	1722		Liverpool L.S.	31.407
1M19	0922		Liverpool L.S.	31.406	1M42	1743	SUN	Liverpool L.S.	31.415
1M32	1022		Liverpool L.S.	31.410	1E85	1815	SUN	Norwich	31.418
1M30	1122		Liverpool L.S.	31.407	1M57	1858	SUN	Liverpool L.S.	31.412
1M39	1155	SUN	Liverpool L.S.	31.417	1M61	1922		Liverpool L.S.	31.405
1M44	1222		Liverpool L.S.	31.411	1M56	2122		Liverpool L.S.	31.409
1M33	1422		Liverpool L.S.	31.401	1M60	2201	SUN	Liverpool L.S.	31.413

Sherborne

1O13	0845	SX	Waterloo	33.107

Shrewsbury

1A13	0709	SX	Euston	47.453	1A63	1531		Euston	47.453 86.203
1A41	1133		Euston	47.453 86.213					47.429 86.202
				47.429 86.244	1A33	1733	SUN	Euston	47.457 86.268
1A28	1426	SUN	Euston	47.457 86.438	1E24	2250	SX	York	47.543

Skipton

2P00	0600	SX	Carlisle	47.642

Southampton C.

1V02	0155		Bristol T.M.	33.014	1M17	1548	SUN	Liverpool L.S.	47.572 86.437
1S39	1148	SUN	Glasgow C.	86.442	1M40	1816	SUN	Manchester P.	47.568 47.569
1E63	1448	SUN	Newcastle	47.416 47.485					

Stafford

1H02	0205		Manchester P.	86.201	1F10	0845		Liverpool L.S.	86.204
1H02	0249	SUN	Manchester P.	47.464	1V87	1609		Paddington	47.541

Stirling

1P02	0548		Edinburgh	47.511

Stranraer Hbr.

1A02	0700		Glasgow C.	47.510	1A06	1835	SUN	Glasgow C.	47.660
1M06	1055		Euston	47.591 86.227	1M14	2240		Euston	47.593 86.406
1A04	1425		Glasgow C.	47.509					86.242
1A06	1835		Glasgow C.	47.510 47.596					

Swansea

1M70	0745		Manchester P.	47.550	1O46	1605		Portsmouth Hbr.	33.002 37.402
1O40	0950		Portsmouth Hbr.	33.003 37.402					47.563
				47.563	1A71	1640	SUN	Paddington	47.580
1A53	1245	SUN	Paddington	47.581	1M82	1828	SUN	Crewe	37.406

Swindon

1C11	0645		Penzance	50.028	2C13	0726		Taunton	50.027

Taunton

2C71	1000		Bristol T.M.	50.027	2C85	1900		Bristol T.M.	50.023

Thurso

2H70	0602		Georgemas Jn.	37.421	2H74	1802		Georgemas Jn.	37.421
2H72	1202		Georgemas Jn.	37.421					

Totnes

2C32	0640		Exeter St. D.	50.020

Twyford

1F09	0743	SX	Paddington	50.005

Victoria

2D50	0015	7	Gatwick Airport	73.104	1D66	0615	7	Gatwick Airport	73.104
1D60	0530	7	Gatwick Airport	73.101	1D68	0630	7	Gatwick Airport	73.105
1D62	0545	7	Gatwick Airport	73.102	1D70	0645	7	Gatwick Airport	73.106
1D64	0600	7	Gatwick Airport	73.103	1D72	0700	7	Gatwick Airport	73.107

1D74	0715	7	Gatwick Airport	73.101
1D76	0730	7	Gatwick Airport	73.102
1D78	0745	7	Gatwick Airport	73.103
1D80	0800	7	Gatwick Airport	73.104
1D82	0815	7	Gatwick Airport	73.105
1D84	0830	7	Gatwick Airport	73.106
1D86	0845	7	Gatwick Airport	73.107
1D88	0900	7	Gatwick Airport	73.101
1D90	0915	7	Gatwick Airport	73.102
1D92	0930	7	Gatwick Airport	73.103
1D94	0945	7	Gatwick Airport	73.104
1D00	1000	7	Gatwick Airport	73.105
1D02	1015	7	Gatwick Airport	73.106
1D04	1030	7	Gatwick Airport	73.107
1D06	1045	7	Gatwick Airport	73.101
1D08	1100	7	Gatwick Airport	73.102
1D10	1115	7	Gatwick Airport	73.103
1D12	1130	7	Gatwick Airport	73.104
1D14	1145	7	Gatwick Airport	73.105
1D16	1200	7	Gatwick Airport	73.106
1D18	1215	7	Gatwick Airport	73.107
1D20	1230	7	Gatwick Airport	73.101
1D22	1245	7	Gatwick Airport	73.102
1D24	1300	7	Gatwick Airport	73.103
1D26	1315	7	Gatwick Airport	73.104
1D28	1330	7	Gatwick Airport	73.105
1D30	1345	7	Gatwick Airport	73.106
1D32	1400	7	Gatwick Airport	73.107
1D34	1415	7	Gatwick Airport	73.101
1D36	1430	7	Gatwick Airport	73.102
1D38	1445	7	Gatwick Airport	73.103
1D40	1500	7	Gatwick Airport	73.104
1D42	1515	7	Gatwick Airport	73.105
1D44	1530	7	Gatwick Airport	73.106
1D46	1545	7	Gatwick Airport	73.107
1D48	1600	7	Gatwick Airport	73.101
1D50	1615	7	Gatwick Airport	73.102
1D52	1630	7	Gatwick Airport	73.103
1D54	1645	7	Gatwick Airport	73.104
1D56	1700	7	Gatwick Airport	73.105
1D58	1715	7	Gatwick Airport	73.106
1D60	1730	7	Gatwick Airport	73.107
1D62	1745	7	Gatwick Airport	73.101
1D64	1800	7	Gatwick Airport	73.102
1D66	1815	7	Gatwick Airport	73.103
1D68	1830	7	Gatwick Airport	73.104
1D70	1845	7	Gatwick Airport	73.105
1D72	1900	7	Gatwick Airport	73.106
1D74	1915	7	Gatwick Airport	73.107
1D76	1930	7	Gatwick Airport	73.101
1D78	1945	7	Gatwick Airport	73.102
1D80	2000	7	Gatwick Airport	73.103
1D82	2015	7	Gatwick Airport	73.104
1D84	2030	7	Gatwick Airport	73.105
1D86	2045	7	Gatwick Airport	73.106
1D88	2100	7	Gatwick Airport	73.107
1D90	2115	7	Gatwick Airport	73.101
1D92	2130	7	Gatwick Airport	73.102
1D94	2145	7	Gatwick Airport	73.103
1D00	2200	7	Gatwick Airport	73.104
1D04	2230	7	Gatwick Airport	73.106
1D08	2300	7	Gatwick Airport	73.101
1D12	2300	7	Gatwick Airport	73.102

Waterloo

1V01	0130	SUN	Yeovil Jn.	33.035	50.043
1V01	0130	SUN	Salisbury	50.043	
1V01	0130	SUN	Yeovil Jn.	50.019	50.015
1Y01	0200	SUN	Fareham	33.032	
1Y01	0245	SX	Portsmouth Hbr.	33.003	
1B01	0245		Bournemouth	33.101	33.108
1Y01	0245	SO	Portsmouth Hbr.	33.018	
1P03	0315	SUN	Portsmouth & S.	33.025	
1P05	0340	SUN	Petersfield	73.123	
1W05	0540		Weymouth	33.103	
1W07	0644		Weymouth	33.102	
1V07	0700		Exeter St. D.	50.021	
1B03	0744		Bournemouth	73.109	
1L03	0810	SX	Salisbury	33.105	
1W11	0830	SUN	Weymouth	33.116	
1W11	0832		Weymouth	33.101	
1W13	0844	SUN	Weymouth	33.109	
1V09	0910		Exeter St. D.	50.016	
1V09	0910	SUN	Exeter St. D.	50.041	
1V09	0910	SUN	Honiton	50.041	
1P15	0925	SX	Portsmouth Hbr.	50.019	
1W15	0930	SUN	Weymouth	33.109	
1W13	0932		Weymouth	33.103	
1W21	0944	SUN	Weymouth	33.111 73.120	33.112
1L05	1010		Salisbury	33.106	
1W21	1032		Weymouth	33.102	
1B13	1044		Bournemouth	73.110	
1W23	1044	SUN	Weymouth	33.111	33.112
1V11	1110		Exeter St. D.	50.015	
1V11	1110	SUN	Exeter St. D.	50.039	50.039
1W23	1132		Weymouth	33.101	
1B17	1144		Bournemouth	73.112	
1W29	1144	SUN	Weymouth	33.116	
1L07	1210		Salisbury	33.107	
1W29	1232		Weymouth	33.103	
1B19	1244		Bournemouth	73.111	
1W31	1244	SUN	Weymouth	33.109	
1V13	1310		Exeter St. D.	50.018	
1W31	1332		Weymouth	33.102	
1B21	1344		Bournemouth	73.109	
1W33	1344	SUN	Weymouth	33.111	
1L09	1410		Salisbury	33.015	33.106
1V14	1410	SUN	Exeter St. D.	50.043	
1W33	1432		Weymouth	33.101	
1W37	1444	SUN	Weymouth	33.116	
1V15	1510		Exeter St. D.	50.020	
1W37	1532		Weymouth	33.103	
1B27	1544	SX	Bournemouth	73.114	
1B27	1544	SUN	Bournemouth	73.120	
1L11	1610	SO	Salisbury	33.021	
1W39	1630	SUN	Weymouth	33.109	
1W39	1632		Weymouth	33.102	
1V16	1642	SX	Exeter St. D.	50.017	
1B29	1644	SO	Bournemouth	73.110	
1B29	1644	SUN	Bournemouth	73.119	
2L31	1700	SX	Basingstoke	33.107	
1V17	1710	SO	Exeter St. D.	50.031	
1V17	1710	SUN	Exeter St. D.	50.040	
1B31	1716	SX	Bournemouth	73.110	
1W41	1730	SX	Weymouth	33.101	
1W41	1730	SUN	Weymouth	33.111	
1W41	1732	SO	Weymouth	33.101	
1V17	1738	SX	Exeter St. D.	50.021	
1B33	1744	SO	Bournemouth	73.112	
1B33	1744	SUN	Bournemouth	73.118	
1V18	1810	SX	Yeovil Jn.	33.106	
1L13	1810	SO	Salisbury	33.107	
1W43	1830	SUN	Weymouth	33.112	73.122
1W43	1832		Weymouth	33.103	33.103
1B35	1844		Bournemouth	73.111	
1V19	1910		Exeter St. D.	50.014	50.021
1V19	1910	SUN	Exeter St. D.	50.044	
1W45	1930	SUN	Weymouth	33.109	
1W45	1932		Weymouth	33.102	
1B37	1944	SX	Bournemouth	73.109	
1V20	2010	SUN	Exeter St. D.	50.041	
1V20	2038		Yeovil Jn.	50.016	
1W49	2044		Weymouth	33.101	33.108
1W49	2044	SUN	Weymouth	33.111	

1V21	2110	SUN	Yeovil Jn.	33.029 50.039
1B39	2144	SX	Bournemouth	73.114
1L15	2210		Salisbury	50.015 33.022
1L15	2210	SUN	Salisbury	33.029 50.039

1W53	2244	SUN	Weymouth	33.103
1W55	2252		Weymouth	33.103 33.015
				73.108
1W55	2252	SUN	Weymouth	33.109

Westbury

1F15	0647	SX	Paddington	50.009
1O35	1046	SUN	Portsmouth Hbr.	33.023
1B27	1200	SUN	Cardiff C.	33.024
1O40	1247	SUN	Portsmouth Hbr.	33.037

1B31	1400	SUN	Bristol T.M.	33.028
1O42	1444	SUN	Portsmouth Hbr.	33.034
2O97	2247	SO	Salisbury	33.010

Weston Super Mare

2C79	1750		Bristol T.M.	47.414 47.553
				50.027

1A90	2040	SUN	Paddington	47.574

Weymouth

1W04	0609	SX	Waterloo	33.103 73.110
1W04	0632	SO	Waterloo	33.103
1W08	0730	SX	Waterloo	33.102
1W08	0732	SO	Waterloo	33.102
2W02	0806	SX	Bournemouth	33.104
1W14	0821	SUN	Waterloo	33.109 33.116
1W14	0833		Waterloo	33.101
1W14	0848	SUN	Waterloo	33.109
1W16	0932		Waterloo	33.103
1W16	0951	SUN	Waterloo	33.111 33.112
1W22	1032		Waterloo	33.102
1W22	1034	SUN	Waterloo	33.111 33.112
1W24	1132		Waterloo	33.101
1W24	1140	SUN	Waterloo	33.116 73.120
1W28	1228		Waterloo	33.103
1W28	1251	SUN	Waterloo	33.109
1W30	1332		Waterloo	33.102
1W30	1348	SUN	Waterloo	33.111 33.112
1W32	1430	SUN	Waterloo	33.111
1W32	1432		Waterloo	33.101
1W32	1451	SUN	Waterloo	33.112
1W34	1530	SUN	Waterloo	33.116

1W34	1532		Waterloo	33.103
1W38	1630	SUN	Waterloo	33.109
1W38	1631	SX	Waterloo	33.102
1W38	1632	SO	Waterloo	33.102
1W42	1726	SUN	Waterloo	33.111
1W42	1733	SX	Waterloo	33.101
1W42	1737	SO	Waterloo	33.101
1W44	1851	SUN	Waterloo	33.116
1W44	1854	SO	Waterloo	33.103
1W44	1902	SX	Waterloo	33.103
2V70	1935		Bristol T.M.	33.005
1W46	1946	SO	Waterloo	33.102
1W46	1948	SUN	Waterloo	33.109
1W46	1954	SX	Waterloo	33.102
1W48	2051	SUN	Waterloo	33.111
2W06	2100		Bournemouth	33.101
1W50	2238		Waterloo	50.016 33.104
2W10	2242	SUN	Bournemouth	33.109
1W50	2253	SO	Eastleigh	33.103
2W08	2338	SO	Dorchester S.	33.102
1W52	2348	SUN	Poole	33.112

Wick

2H60	0600		Inverness	37.423
2H62	1200		Inverness	37.424

2H64	1800		Inverness	37.423

Wolverhampton

1E62	0520		Harwich P.Q.	31.405
1A72	0556		Euston	86.227 86.247
1A05	0630	SX	Euston	86.231
1O01	0645		Poole	47.454
1A07	0656		Euston	87.014 86.232
1O66	0700	SUN	Brighton	47.566 86.263
1A09	0726	SX	Euston	87.025
2G80	0734		Birmingham N.S.	31.403 31.426
1A13	0756		Euston	87.002
1A05	0800	SUN	Euston	86.265
1A17	0826	SX	Euston	86.203
1A06	0900	SUN	Euston	86.269
1A14	0926		Euston	86.221 87.028
1A08	1000	SUN	Euston	87.035
1A36	1126		Euston	86.206
1A44	1256	SO	Euston	86.242

1A46	1326	SX	Euston	86.215
1A50	1326	SO	Euston	87.004
1A12	1335	SUN	Euston	86.275
1A50	1426		Euston	87.004 86.243
1A20	1430	SUN	Euston	86.250
1A57	1526		Euston	86.201 87.017
1A25	1556	SUN	Euston	87.054
1A65	1656		Euston	87.005 86.233
1A48	1656	SUN	Euston	86.265
1A68	1726		Euston	86.206 86.201
1A74	1826		Euston	87.022 86.428
1A84	2026		Euston	86.213 86.204
1A85	2026	SUN	Euston	86.262
1A42	2156	FSX	Euston	86.210
1V20	2235	SX	Oxford	50.004

Yarmouth

1M31	0750		Liverpool L.S.	31.409 31.409
				31.422

1P23	0810		Liverpool St.	31.423
2P77	1820		Norwich	31.421 31.404

Yeovil Jn.

2O91	0510	SO	Salisbury	50.015
2O91	0515	SX	Salisbury	50.019
2O91	0723	SUN	Salisbury	33.035

2O94	2120	SX	Basingstoke	33.106 33.106
				33.107

Yeovil P.M.

2C16	0655		Bristol T.M.	33.006

York

1V89	1317	SUN	Weston Super Mare	47.574

1M41	2225	SX	Shrewsbury	47.544

5 × 8 -
50.